take 2

s for Rescued Dogs

BY JOEL SILVERMAN

Lead Editor: Amy Deputato
Editor: Jarelle S. Stein
Consulting Editor: Babette Haggerty
Senior Art Director: Véronique Bos
Graphic Designer: Kelley Pelton
Production Coordinators: Tracy Burns, Jessica Jaensch
Publishing Coordinator: Karen Julian

Vice President, Chief Content Officer: June Kikuchi
Vice President, Kennel Club Books: Andrew DePrisco
BowTie Press: Jennifer Calvert, Amy Deputato, Lindsay Hanks,
Karen Julian, Elizabeth L. McCaughey, Roger Sipe, Jarelle S. Stein

Kennel Club Books®
A Division of BowTie, Inc.
40 Broad Street
Freehold, NJ 07728 • USA
www.kennelclubbooks.com

Library of Congress Cataloging-in-Publication Data

Silverman, Joel, 1958-.
Take 2 : training solutions for rescued dogs / by Joel Silverman.
p. cm.
Includes index.
ISBN 978-1-59378-639-7
1. Dog adoption. 2. Dog rescue. 3. Dogs--Training. 4. Dogs--Behavior. I. Title. II. Title: Take two.
SF427.S5945 2010
636.7'0887--dc22
2010028470

Printed and bound in China
14 13 12 11 10   1 2 3 4 5 6 7 8 9 10

contents

acknowledgments

Any book is the work of many people, and any dog book is the work of many people and dogs. Because the dogs aren't editing me, I will start with the people. My thanks to the editors at BowTie Press, especially Andrew DePrisco, Amy Deputato, Babette Haggerty, and Jarelle Stein, and to publishing coordinator Karen Julian, who also served as a model for our training photo shoots.

Thanks to my good friend, the amazing photographer Fernando Escovar, whose work is seen on the cover of this book, and to Pam Marks, whose images grace the interior.

Thanks to Mission Viejo Animal Services Center, Melissa Kauffman, and Lisa MacDonald, who so graciously volunteered their facilities and homes for our photo shoots, and to Autumn Ewoldt of Cedar Bend Humane Society and Pam Wiese of Nebraska Humane Society for sharing their photos with us.

A much-deserved shout-out to my good friend Bryan Renfro, who shared many of his dog-training techniques with me three decades ago—and I share them with you.

Heartfelt thanks goes to the owners of our cover dogs: my good friend of thirty years, Steve Berens of Animals of Distinction, and Beth Javier.

Last but not least, I thank all of our cover dogs, especially my own companion, Foster, whom I rescued from the Orange County Animal Shelter; Ted the Chihuahua; and Abbey the German Shepherd Dog, star of the motion picture *I Am Legend*, trained by Steve Berens.

The publisher would like to thank the following photographers and other providers of photos for this book:

absolut/Shutterstock
Yuri Arcurs/Shutterstock
Noam Armonn/Shutterstock
AVAVA/Shutterstock
Stephane Bidouze/Shutterstock
Steve Brigman/Shutterstock
Cedar Bend Humane Society
Cioli & Hunnicutt/BowTie
Willee Cole/Shutterstock
cynoclub/Shutterstock
David Davis/Shutterstock
sonya etchison/Shutterstock
Mars Evis/Shutterstock
George Fairbairn
Isabelle Francais
Gorilla/Shutterstock
Kimberly Hall/Shutterstock
Susan Harris/Shutterstock
HomeStudio/Shutterstock
IKO/Shutterstock
Julien/Shutterstock
Karkas/Shutterstock
Dmitry Kramar/Shutterstock
Sergey Lavrentev/Shutterstock
marikond/Shutterstock
Pam Marks
matabum/Shutterstock
Michelle D. Milliman/Shutterstock
Nebraska Humane Society
Neeila/Shutterstock
Tomas Pavelka/Shutterstock
Anita Patterson Peppers/Shutterstock
Maxim Petrichuk/Shutterstock
Photosani/Shutterstock
plastique/Shutterstock
saasemen/Shutterstock
S_E/Shutterstock
Konstantin Shevtsov/Shutterstock
Joel Silverman
Wendy M. Simmons/Shutterstock
Smart-foto/Shutterstock
Michaela Stejskalova/Shutterstock
April Turner/Shutterstock
Svetlana Valoueva/Shutterstock
Anke van Wyk/Shutterstock
Emily Veinglory/Shutterstock
Ivonne Wierink/Shutterstock
Yeko Photo Studio/Shutterstock
yui/Shutterstock

introduction
take 2

"Zulu" once belonged to Fred and Catherine. His former daddy, Fred, manages a retail store in a large outlet mall, and his former mommy, Catherine, is a bookkeeper for a local plumbing business. (Zulu never knew any of that, by the way.) College sweethearts, the newlyweds still enjoy a great social life with their many mutual friends and their work associates.

Zulu is the Shih Tzu puppy they received as a gift from a college pal. When Fred and Catherine met this irresistible bundle of auburn fluff, both new pet parents were over the moon.

Once reality set in, Zulu spent long periods of time in her crate while Fred and Catherine worked and played. Time with the noontime dog walker was the highlight of Zulu's day. When her parents came home, usually late in the evening, her joy was expressed in yips, yaps, and inevitable puddles. The couple didn't much mind, or even notice, the wee for the first few months, but after a while Fred's patience wore thin and Catherine stopped making excuses. Zulu was impossible to house-train, they agreed.

The animal shelter on Main Street is great with rehoming toy dogs, and they're sure that Zulu will find a better home in just a few days.

A comical terrier mix, "Homer" is five years old and once had a human baby sister named Sandy and two parents, George and Amulya. A few years after George and Amulya got married, Homer joined their family. Having grown up with dogs, George used to call him "the kid" or "daddy's boy," which always made Amulya roll her eyes and wonder. Homer was the first dog Amulya had ever owned.

When the squirmy, gurgling Sandy arrived, Homer was all grown up, though still a bit gawky, with legs that seemed to belong to a much larger dog. He enjoyed listening to Sandy's baby sounds and liked watching his parents play with the new installment.

Sandy didn't start paying much attention to Homer until she started toddling around the house. George and Amulya enjoyed seeing their two "babies" interact with each other, and "daddy's boy" enjoyed playing with his now two-year-old sister. He didn't even mind Sandy's clumsy attempts at petting—really more grabbing and pulling than petting—but as soon as the toddler would latch on to his sensitive ears or long tail, the game would quickly end.

One day, when a warning growl failed, Homer retreated from the playroom to the safety of his parents. When Sandy chased him into the kitchen, Homer turned around and followed the growl with a snap in her direction.

Standing at the stove, Amulya panicked. "This dog's become unpredictable, George," she said, "and the baby is at risk."

After days of watching Homer's every move and pleading with his wife to change her mind, George tearfully dropped Homer off at a no-kill shelter.

• •

"Trump," a Goldendoodle, was a needy soul by anyone's definition, though his former parents never saw it. Jessica and Rob both had major careers on Wall Street. Commuting downtown and working long hours in the office meant that their usual "9 to 5" was more like "7 to 7." A true yuppy puppy whose "designer mix" had been featured in the *New York Times*, Trump went to doggy daycare three days a week and had a dog walker take him out twice a day on his days at home. He enjoyed attention from everyone he met, especially when Jessica and Rob let him tag along on their weekend hikes.

For all Trump's cuddly cuteness, Jessica and Rob were unresponsive to his overtures. He was a good boy, naturally obedient, happy to please. In their minds, though, he was just a bit dopey and not very driven. They had had such great expectations for their Goldendoodle, whom they named after The Donald.

When the economy began to slump, Trump's parents became less interested in the dog. Doggy daycare was cut back to once a week, and their weekend outings dried up. Jessica lost her job. Soon thereafter, Rob's company decided to move him to Chicago, and the couple had no choice but to relocate quickly.

The apartment they could find in Naperville, on the outskirts of Chicago, did not accept dogs. Trump was surrendered to an all-breed rescue group before the move.

• •

Perhaps you're about to become a new parent for a Zulu, a Homer, or a Trump. If you're planning to adopt or already have adopted or rescued a dog, you may be giving a second chance to a worthy dog whose first parents were less than ideal. Many "Take 2" dogs do come from homes in which their owners didn't take the time to house-train them, or give them proper supervision around the children, or even take the time to get to know them. While not all adopted dogs come with problems, they do come with a past, be it good or bad; that past—whatever they experienced in their previous homes—has shaped them up to this point.

From my 2009 book tour of the United States—some 20,000 miles through 100 cities in thirty-eight states—I learned that too many people simply lack the education that is required to own a dog. These folks aren't uncaring or bad people; they just don't know what's required to be good dog owners.

If you're reading this book, I'm assuming that you've decided (or are about to decide) to adopt a dog from an animal shelter, rescue group, or humane society. Rescuing a great dog is the right thing to do in light of the animal overpopulation problem that exists in most places these days.

The purpose of *Take 2* is to educate as many people as possible. My desire to teach people how to be better dog owners, to show people how to better train their dogs, and to improve the lives of dogs everywhere is what fuels my motor home as I visit the Lower 48. (If Hawaii and Alaska invite me, by the way, I'm there!)

In the course of one year, I met hundreds of thousands of people at pet expos, doggy daycare centers, professional seminars, and training centers as well as at humane societies and animal shelters.

So many kindhearted dog-loving folk are out there, looking for direction, and together we can solve any problem—from house-training setbacks and aggressive behavior to the overcrowding in shelters around the country.

At the risk of sounding like a 1960s demonstrator or a flower child at Woodstock, I can tell you that what we really need is L-O-V-E! It all starts with love—bonding with a dog, getting to know him, and building a relationship of trust and patience. That is what's required to earn the love of man's (and woman's) best friend.

As we all know, too many dogs are surrendered and destroyed every year. If people followed my simple rules of dog ownership and training, fewer and fewer canine friends would end up homeless or, worse, dead. It's unimaginable to me, as a true dog lover and a longtime dog trainer, that people surrender these selfless, feeling creatures to strangers (albeit caring strangers, most of them). But we must all accept it as a reality, for now, and be brave new owners ready for "Take 2."

In this book, I am going to spell out a game plan for you to use to train your adopted dog. I want to lay the foundation of understanding that you will need to build the best possible relationship with your dog. Once you've done that, training can begin. In fact, you can only really train an animal that trusts you, whether it's a Chihuahua or a killer whale. (I have trained both. Chihuahuas are much harder!)

Except for very young puppies, every adopted dog has some baggage. We humans have it, after all, and so do our canine friends! And like us, some have more than others, of course. That baggage can affect how an adopted dog initially responds to his new owners and to any training. Say, for example, that you are trying to train that newly adopted Chihuahua before you get to know him. He's acting shy and timid, but you try to force a behavior (such as *sit* or *down*) on him, which causes him to become more timid or possibly even show fear aggression. The wrong kind of training can aggravate his behavioral tendencies. This scenario is not uncommon and often ends with the dog being given up by his owners—yet again.

Had the new owner given the little dog some time to come out of his taco shell, the situation would definitely have grown rosier. The dog begins to trust his new owner and begins to show a desire to please his new owner, and effective training takes root. (A note to my

Chihuahua pals out there: I love Chihuahuas and mean no offense with this example. I've trained lots of smart Chihuahuas.)

How do you prevent Take 2 from becoming Take 3? Deciding to adopt a rescue dog requires a game plan, something that likely was lacking in the dog's first household. We don't want your enthusiasm to "do the right thing" to turn into "adding insult to injury." It's unfortunate enough for Zulu, Homer, and Trump to have been turned into a shelter once; a second time would be tragic—and certainly is avoidable.

Before stepping onto the court or field, every person has to evaluate what he or she is bringing to the game. Are you ready for this match of dog ownership? I'm sure that thousands fewer dogs would be sitting in shelters tonight if more people had really thought about whether they were ready for a dog before taking one home. I'm also sure that most of the dogs in shelters got there by no fault of their own—the fault rests squarely on the shoulders of the people who threw in the towel, who did not give these dogs enough attention and affection, who didn't have a game plan.

So think long and carefully before you make the decision to adopt a dog. Ask yourself if this the best time for you to take on this responsibility. Do you have the time to train, walk, and play with your new dog? Are you ready to lavish love and attention on him? Is every member of household preparing to make the changes necessary to keep your dog safe? Only when you can answer "yes" to those questions should you move forward.

Once you are ready, this book will help you and your family take the next steps toward adopting a dog from a shelter, a humane society, or a rescue group. I will tell you what you can expect when you are looking at or meeting a dog, tell you what you need to know about the actual adoption, and, most importantly, give you a minute-by-minute game plan for that very first day with your new friend.

Later in the book, I offer you hands-on advice about most of the major problems that owners of adopted dogs encounter in the first few weeks and months after the dog comes home, from separation anxiety and house-training issues to escaping and destructiveness.

Yes, of course, there will be problems. Are you still sure you're ready? If so, then let's Take 2!

finding your new dog

When a guy discovers someone or something that he really likes, no stretch of highway is too great. That's how I feel about my veterinarian, who now lives 90 miles from me. Of course, a long-distance vet is no good for an emergency, but for other types of consultations, it's OK to take a road trip.

In 2005, my dog Ellis was having a recurring knee problem, and I made an appointment with my vet to check him out. Had I not traveled down to southern Orange County to visit the doc, I would never have wandered into the animal shelter there and found my awesome dog Foster. I wasn't necessarily looking for a dog, but I had time to kill while I waited for Ellis.

Many dog lovers aren't comfortable in animal shelters because shelters can be stark, noisy, and not always cheery. I am, however, because I visit them often. Throughout my career as an animal trainer, I have visited countless adoption facilities around the country, holding seminars with trainers, new owners, and prospective adopters, teaching them about the demands, challenges, and rewards of pet

ownership. That day, I was welcomed by the friendly staff, who remembered me from previous visits.

I began to wander by the cages, greeting the dogs. Then I reached a cage containing a jet-black little mongrel with a white star on his chest. I knelt and put my hand on the bar of his cage about 6 inches from the ground, and he immediately rested his fuzzy chin on my hand and just stared at me. Then, I moved my hand to the other side of the cage, and he rushed over and again rested his chin on my hand. With each round of this new game, Foster's stare grew more intense as he willed me to take him home. Although I hadn't planned on adopting a dog that day, Foster basically stared me down until I gave in.

Ellis, an accomplished animal actor trained by the author. PREVIOUS PAGE: Foster today is a well-adjusted, well-traveled star performer.

While Foster and I got to know each other in the visiting area, I asked the shelter volunteers about his background. Other than the fact that he had been picked up as a stray, they knew very little about him. They thought he was probably some kind of terrier mix and estimated his age at six to eight months. If I wanted to know anything else about Foster, I would have to discover it for myself.

Once I got Foster home, I found out that his idea of house-training was to pee quickly on the furniture and then run! I surmised from his unrefined manners and complete lack of social skills that he had never been trained. He also had a curious aversion to brooms, mops, and anything with a long handle. From that, I concluded that Foster had most likely been mistreated. (A person who would discipline a dog with a broom doesn't deserve to have a dog or any other pet.) This future flawless animal actor had an unpredictable aggressive streak as well and would snap at people or objects without warning or provocation (another indication of possible abuse).

I don't mean this to sound corny, but the first thing I gave this little furry menace was love. It is clearly what he lacked in his first home (along with the obvious house-training lessons), and it's what

I believe all dog owners must serve up in heaping scoops when they start training their dogs. If the dog feels like he's loved and wanted, he'll love in return and want to work with and for his owner.

This experience at an animal shelter isn't completely typical. Most people can't wander into a shelter and leave with a future superstar—or any dog, for that matter—the very same day. But great stories and happy endings begin at animal shelters, humane societies, and rescue groups every day. Let's see what's involved in making yours happen.

Humane Societies, Animal Shelters, and Rescue Groups

Let's begin with the three main kinds of organizations from which you can adopt a dog: animal shelters, humane societies, and rescue groups. Before you decide to adopt a dog from one of these sources, you should know a little about each one and be acquainted with some of the differences between them.

As a trainer of animals for movies, TV shows, and commercials, I would say that over 90 percent of the mixed-breed dogs you see on the big screen and little screen were adopted from one of these organizations. Many trainers in the entertainment business have adopted not only mixed-breed dogs but also some great purebred future canine actors.

ANIMAL SHELTERS

Having adopted many dogs from animal shelters, I've always been a huge supporter of these wonderful organizations. Animal shelters are facilities run by city or county governments, funded by your tax dollars. Although an animal shelter may not look as attractive as some humane societies do, you'll find the same kind of hardworking and caring individuals there. Animal shelters usually have few paid employees—maybe several animal-control officers, a kennel helper or two, and an administrative person to assist with adoptions and paperwork, while volunteers pitch in to help with the rest. "Friends of the shelter" volunteer groups often form to help with fund-raising and to provide services such as dog walking, cleaning, meeting with prospective adopters, and just plain spending time with the animals, giving them attention and socialization.

After visiting shelters and talking with some of the people who work there, I can tell you that being a shelter worker is a tough job, and it can be hard for the people to come into work every day. Shelters often face the problem of overcrowding, and when they run out of space, they may need to euthanize adoptable animals to make room for new arrivals. And when conditions and policies such as these are beyond their control, it makes the workers' jobs even more difficult.

A soft bed, a warm blanket, and some toys help this dog feel comfortable while he awaits his forever family.

'Net Pets

Petfinder.com is a popular Web site that serves as a sort of online adoption clearinghouse, listing close to 300,000 available pets from over 13,000 adoption organizations nationwide, including animal shelters, humane societies, purebred. rescues, and all-dog rescues. You can search for organizations in your area and browse photos and descriptions of their adoptable dogs, or you can narrow your search by specifying a given breed; the search results will return only dogs of that breed or dogs with that breed in their mix. When you find a dog in whom you're interested, you can then contact the organization's adoption coordinator for more information or to schedule a visit, or you can visit the organization's Web site to learn about their adoption polices and fees. Petfinder also offers helpful information on adoption, animal care, pet health, adoption events, training, and more. The Petfinder Foundation works with organizations across the country to provide funding, supplies, and training with the goal of reducing the rate of euthanasia.

Dogs can end up in shelters for many reasons; for example, they may be surrendered by their owners or they may be picked up as strays by animal-control officers. In some cases, they may be removed from their owners due to neglect or abuse, but this is true of only a small percentage of shelter dogs. Depending on the size of your local shelter, you might see more than one dog sharing a kennel there.

Regardless of what an animal shelter looks like, the dogs there are no different from the dogs you will find for adoption anywhere else. They are all simply looking for good, loving homes.

HUMANE SOCIETIES

Humane societies are funded by private donations and run by individuals, not by city or county governments. A privately run humane society is different than the Humane Society of the United States (HSUS). Private humane organizations do great things for animals and do excellent jobs of encouraging responsible pet ownership.

Because humane societies are privately funded, you will see a wide range in their facilities as well as in the services they provide.

Sometimes space limitations necessitate multiple dogs per run. Other times, bonded dogs who come in together stay together.

For example, some are storefront locations or very small buildings with little or no property, while others have spacious buildings on large pieces of land. Some humane societies can house only a few animals, while others can house a few hundred. A humane society's staff may comprise volunteers only or a combination of volunteers and paid employees. Some humane societies are able to have veterinarians and trainers on staff. The operation of a humane society may be overseen by several individuals, or there may be a board of directors who makes the decisions.

On the facing page, you will see one of the larger humane societies in the United States, the Nebraska Humane Society in Omaha, Nebraska, as well as the Cedar Bend Humane Society in Waterloo, Iowa, which is a much smaller facility. Both of these are run by some very remarkable individuals, and I have had a great relationship with these organizations, as well as with dozens of others, for a number of years.

The front of the spacious new adoption center at Cedar Bend Humane Society. Indoors, a separate room houses puppies and small dogs.

Visitors to Nebraska Humane Society are greeted by a large, inviting lobby and a staffed information desk.

The get-acquainted room at Nebraska Humane's adoption facility is an indoor area where dogs and prospective owners can meet and spend some time together.

RESCUE GROUPS

Rescue groups vary greatly when it comes to where they house the dogs and what types of dogs they have for adoption. Some rescues operate much like humane societies, housing all of their dogs at a given location. The type of rescue with which I am most familiar, though, is that which operates through a network of foster homes. The dogs do not live in kennels or shelter facilities but in homes with foster families until they are adopted.

Some rescue groups will have a wide variety of dogs—different types of purebreds as well as mixed-breed dogs—available for adoption. Other rescue groups focus on specific breeds. Many of the national breed clubs have rescue groups associated with them; other breed-specific rescues are independently run. For the more popular breeds in the country, such as the German Shepherd Dog, Labrador and Golden Retrievers, Shih Tzu, and Poodle, there are multiple rescue groups working in conjunction with the breed parent clubs. What's great about these folks is that as rescuers of a particular breed, they should be knowledgeable about their breed and able to answer any of your questions. Most of the breed-specific rescue groups are run by responsible dog breeders. These caring individuals work selflessly

Be Informed

Be informed before you adopt. A second-chance dog deserves a forever home, not another owner who will abandon him if things don't turn out exactly as expected. If you are looking for a specific breed and want to learn more, you can visit my Web site: www.companionsforlife.net. Click on "Purebreds" under "Looking to Adopt," and this will take you to an area where you can read about the breed of dog in which you are interested. Breeds are grouped by size, and once you click on the breed name, you'll find a blurb written by a breeder or a rescuer with specific knowledge of that breed. The writers of these descriptions are people I have met during my career who are very passionate and knowledgeable about their breeds and are willing to share both the pros and cons with prospective owners. Web sites or email addresses are given along with each breed's description in case you have questions or want more information.

for the welfare of all members of their breed, not just the dogs they breed themselves. You can find out about all of the national breed clubs and their associated rescue groups by visiting the American Kennel Club's Web site at www.akc.org.

What I like about rescue groups that house dogs in volunteers' homes is that they give the dogs a better start in a home environment. Dogs fostered with rescue volunteers have the advantage of family interaction, sometimes with children; meeting and socializing with the volunteers' other dogs and pets; and living in a home instead of in a kennel. The dogs have the advantage of one-on-one time with their foster families for leash training, basic cues and manners, grooming, and the like. There is a possibility that a dog coming from a foster situation has already been house-trained or has at least started the process.

By living with a foster dog, a rescuer gets a chance to know the dog, assess his personality, and provide valuable insight into what this dog needs in a new home. Does the dog do well around children? Does he like to play with other dogs? Does he know any basic cues?

In a foster situation, the dog gets to live with a family while the rescuers get to learn about the dog's personality in a home environment.

Does he have any personality quirks or potential behavior issues? Is he a high-energy dog who will do best with an active owner? Based on their observations, foster parents may make recommendations; for example, that a dog be adopted as an "only dog," that the adoptive family has no children under ten years old, or that the dog should go only to a home with a fenced backyard.

In addition to having foster families, rescue groups have volunteers who handle adoption applications, interview prospective adopters, conduct home visits, and coordinate the intake of new dogs when foster space is available. Many rescue groups can exist only through private donations, so fund-raising is another major task of rescue volunteers.

What to Expect

When you arrive to look over the dogs available for adoption or to meet a particular dog, be prepared for what you are about to see and know what you are looking for. You may be going into a crowded kennel building with two or three dogs in every run. If it is nice weather, you may get to see the dogs in outdoor runs. If you are visiting a home in which a person is fostering a rescue dog or if a rescue volunteer is bringing a dog to you for a home visit, you'll be meeting that specific dog because either you or the rescue group think that the dog could be a good match for you.

Foster Homes

If you're thinking about adoption but aren't absolutely sure, you may want to consider fostering a dog for a rescue group. Rescues are always in need of foster homes, because there are always dogs in need of rescue. By fostering, you can take the responsibility of dog ownership for a "test drive." If you find that you aren't ready for a dog, then you have done a good deed by volunteering and have saved yourself some serious trouble.

I mention these things because once an individual or family goes looking for a dog to adopt and starts meeting dogs, they probably will want to save every dog they see. It is essential to go

Breeders: The Bad and the Good

Not all breeders are as giving and caring as the folk who work so diligently for rescue. Some profit-motivated "breeders" are huge factors in dogs' being surrendered to animal shelters, humane societies, and rescue groups, as these people mass-produce puppies with no thought to the dogs' health and welfare. A high percentage of these poorly bred animals have health and temperament problems, and thus end up being abandoned.

On the other hand, I personally know many responsible breeders who have dedicated their lives to their breeds. A responsible breeder does whatever he or she can to reduce the number of dogs in need of rehoming by making each puppy-buyer contractually obligated to return the puppy or grown dog directly to the breeder should the buyer decide that the dog isn't a good fit. These breeders put such verbiage in their contracts because they do not want their animals to be given up to shelters or other adoption organizations. A good breeder will take a dog back and either keep him or oversee his rehoming.

into the adoption process with your head, not your heart. If we all thought with our hearts when we were in an animal shelter, many of us would have fifty dogs. It is important to remind yourself of your wants and must-haves in a dog before you walk inside. Make a commitment to stick to those criteria. Otherwise, you may end up with the neediest dog or the cutest dog, but not a dog who is the right match for you.

ASK QUESTIONS

As the saying goes, there are no stupid questions. It is important to learn as much as possible about the dogs available for adoption, so be ready to ask lots of questions. You'll want to find out as much as you can about the dog's past. However, keep in mind that in some cases not much is known about a dog's history. Even if a dog has been surrendered by his owners, they may not have been completely honest about the dog when they turned him over to the shelter.

In many shelters and humane societies, whatever is known about the dog will be written on a card kept on the door of his kennel. This will usually include age, size, breed or mix, when he came in, and why he came in or where he was found. As the workers get to know the dog better, they may add bits of information about his personality, such as "Pulls on leash" or "Likes belly rubs." This card will be your best source of information about the dog.

If the dog is a mixed breed, and there is no kennel card with information about him, ask what breeds may be in the dog's background. Keep in mind, though, that often a dog's phenotype (what he looks like) is not necessarily indicative of his genotype (what breeds are truly in his DNA). Even if you know what the mix is, you won't know without spending some time with the dog how these breeds have come together to produce his particular temperament. If the dog is a mix of several breeds that you like, then great! But if, for example, you want the laid-back personality of a Basset Hound, you may not be happy with a Basset Hound/Border Collie mix whose temperament is more like the herding-dog side of the family. By contrast, someone who wants an energetic jogging partner will likely be disappointed if the dog exhibits more of the hound's couch-potato tendencies.

If the dog's age is not given, ask someone at the shelter/rescue about it, especially if it's important to you. For many people, age is one of the essential criteria. For example, you may want a mature adult dog without puppy propensities. Some dogs may look like adults at six months old, but they are still puppies and will do all of the things that puppies do, such as chewing on things that you don't want chewed, jumping on people, and barking excessively. A puppy will also need to be house-trained. Adult dogs can still display these and other unwanted behaviors, but for the most part they are calmer than puppies. On the other hand, you may want a puppy or young dog because he has had less time to develop bad habits.

Age also plays a role in the dog's eventual size. With a fully grown adult, you know what size dog you are getting. If you see a puppy who is six months old and weighs 40 pounds, remember that he has a lot more growing to do. Size can be important not only for your personal preferences but also if you live in an apartment complex or other place that puts size restrictions on allowable pets.

If you like a certain purebred dog or a mixed-breed dog who has a high percentage of a specific breed in his ancestry, but you do not know a lot about the breed, get some information from a knowledgeable individual. Don't rely just on the people working at the facility. The best source of information on different breeds is the American Kennel Club. For each of the AKC-recognized breeds, you can find information about size, looks, temperament, history, abilities, and instincts. You'll also find links to each national breed club and contact information for rescue people involved specifically in this breed.

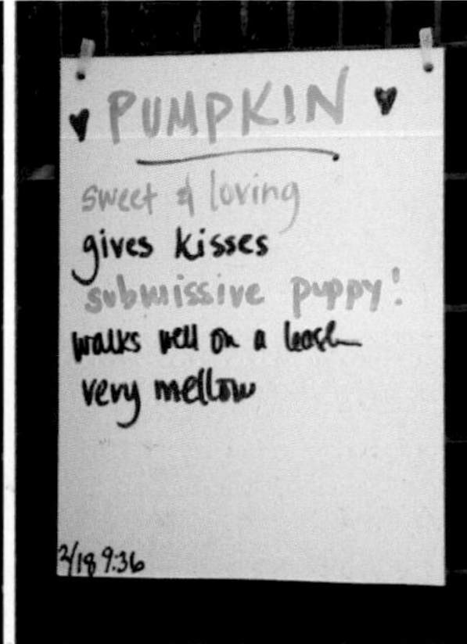

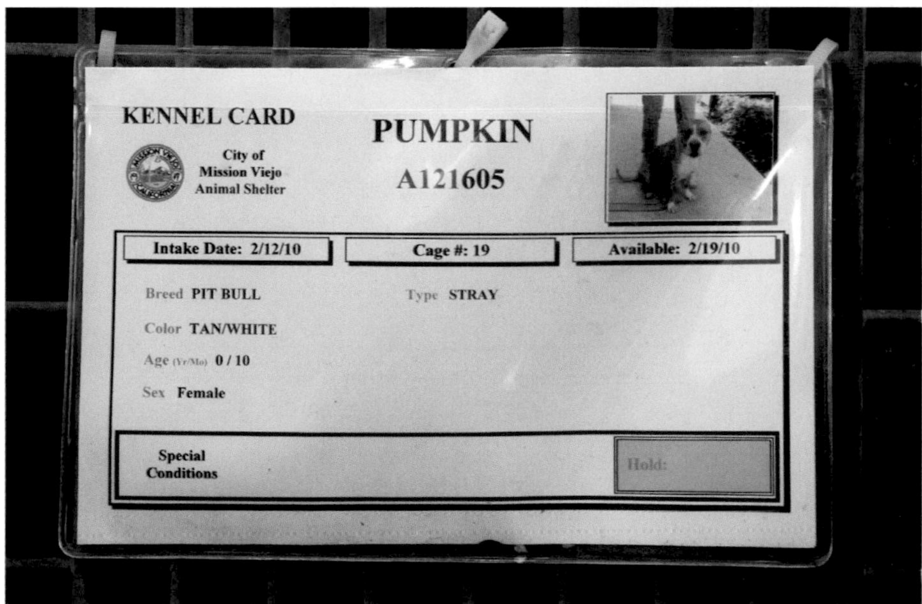

TOP, LEFT: A sign with good news! TOP, RIGHT: A card tells what shelter workers have learned about the dog. BOTTOM: The dog's kennel card lists basic statistics and how the dog came to be at the shelter.

Some of the Lingo

Here are some common terms you may hear as you're meeting different dogs available for adoption:

Stray: If a dog is brought to a shelter or a humane society as a *stray*, it means that the animal was found or picked up by either a citizen or an animal-control officer, not turned in by his previous owners. Dogs become strays for a variety of reasons. Perhaps the dog escaped from his home through a door or a gate accidentally left open. Perhaps he jumped over his backyard fence. Perhaps it was a case of neglect, and the owners just let the dog go. If the dog has no identification and/or is not reclaimed by his owners, he will be made available for adoption. Just remember that, depending on the situation, there is a good possibility that strays are going to need some extra training. You may have an escape artist or a dog with little or no training on your hands. The dog's history will be unknown, and the shelter workers will have to gather information about the dog's behavior and temperament solely through observation.

Surrendered: When a dog is *surrendered*, this means that the person who owned the dog brought him to the facility or rescue group. If the animal is surrendered, there is a good possibility that, for some reason, the animal did not meet the family's criteria (not that this is a valid reason for surrendering a dog!). If the dog is surrendered for a behavioral reason, such as running out the door, snapping, or not being good with other dogs, this information should be written on the dog's kennel card or told to you by the rescuer/foster parent. However, please keep in mind that behavioral issues are not the only reason for a dog's being surrendered. A family may be moving somewhere that does not allow dogs. A person may no longer be able to keep his or her dog due to financial problems. A dog may be surrendered by the owner's family members if the owner dies. The circumstances of the dog's surrender are something you need to be aware of. Some surrendered dogs are great pets right off the bat, and others will become great dogs with some patience, guidance, and training. Some are deemed unadoptable due to aggression issues; for example, a history of biting.

Socialization issues: When a dog's information card or a staff member tells you that a dog "is not good with other dogs," please take it to heart. This information is being shared with you because the animal has a history of problems with other animals. Why is this? We may not know. The dog may have been attacked by a larger dog and has reacted defensively ever since. He may not have been socialized with other dogs and does not know how to react to them properly. Whether or not you know the reasons behind the behavior, don't think this is something you are going to change. You might, over time, be able to socialize him, but remember that some dogs like other dogs, and some don't. There is a chance that you can get the dog to become friendly toward, or at least tolerant of, other dogs as you get to know him and his behavior, and you can even bring in a trainer to help you, but there is never any guarantee.

"Needs a yard": If you are told that a dog "needs a yard," you can take it to mean that the dog has a high energy level and will need ample activity.

"Not enough time": If you are told that the previous owners "didn't have enough time" for the dog, the dog most likely hasn't had much training. If you adopt this dog, you will need to devote time to training him. You can attend obedience classes or work with a private trainer.

A FEW MORE TIPS

I also want to prepare you for asking advice from workers at a busy shelter or humane society. Sometimes a facility is so inundated with dogs that the workers cannot stay updated on each dog. In addition, many of the workers are volunteers who may only be there once or twice a week, so they may not know about new arrivals or may not know the dogs as well as someone who's there every day.

Keep in mind what I mentioned earlier—that owners may not be completely honest about the information they give when they surrender a dog. A great example is my dog Foster, former city shelter resident. I was looking for a dog who was close to fully grown. At the shelter, the card attached to Foster's kennel said that he weighed 10 pounds and was ten months old. Over the next year, he grew to 25 pounds, and his then jet-black coat turned to a beautiful gray. The fact that he more than doubled in sized and his coat changed so much makes it clear that he was not ten months old when I first saw him. He was probably closer to four months old! For me, this was not a big concern, but for some adopters, it might be. The point is to really make sure that you ask questions so you can get as much accurate information on the dog as possible, while bearing in mind that some information may simply be unknown.

Making a Difference

Everyone needs to do his part to decrease the numbers of animals in need of adoption. The individuals who work at and volunteer with animal shelters, humane societies, and rescue groups are doing their part by working to rehome these animals and making sure that every adopted animal is spayed or neutered before going to new homes. Let's all help make a difference!

Meeting the Dog

Once you find a dog who interests you, take full advantage of getting to know him and spending one-on-one time with him. Most places have meet-and-greet areas for dogs and prospective owners. Taking

Being out of his kennel gives the dog a chance to relax and enjoy some attention, which helps his true personality emerge.

the dog to this area gives you a great opportunity to see the dog outside his kennel; the behavior you see when a dog is in his kennel may not necessarily represent the dog's true character.

The dog's history, how long he has been in the shelter, his natural temperament, and the recent changes in his life that brought him to the shelter will affect his attitude at the shelter. By taking the dog to a neutral location, you will get a much better look at his true personality. If the greeting area is an enclosed room indoors, you'll have the chance to take the dog off his leash. If the greeting area is outdoors, a shelter volunteer can accompany you and the dog for an on-leash walk on the shelter grounds. If you're meeting a rescue dog in his foster home, the dog should be more relaxed. You'll learn a lot about the dog by interacting with him, but you'll also gain valuable insight from the foster parents, who have been observing the dog in their home.

Take your time getting to know the dog. Often, you can see some major changes in the dog in as little as twenty minutes. The dog may initially be either a little nervous or a little hyper, but as he adjusts to being out of the kennel and begins to get comfortable with you, you'll get a better idea of what he is really like.

SHY DOGS

A hunched-over posture with the tail tucked between the legs are two body-language signals of a shy dog.

As I mentioned, the first time you make contact with a dog, you might find that he is a little shy or timid. There are a number of signs that will clue you in to this; most of them have to do with the dog's body language. First, notice how the dog is standing. Sometimes, a shy dog will stand a little hunched over, with his head at shoulder height or lower. Take a look at his tail. Is it tucked between his legs? If so, this is another sign of the dog's being shy. Take a look at the dog's ears. A shy dog often holds his ears back and lying flat.

If you do not know much about the dog's history, it will be hard to tell whether he is naturally shy or just uncomfortable in the particular environment or with a person he does not know. It's possible that the way the dog's previous owners treated him has caused him to become timid around people. Can a dog with these characteristics change? Absolutely—but how long it will take really depends on how intense his shyness is and if he also exhibits fear. Some dogs simply need time to warm up, while others need owners who will put some effort into socializing them.

Something else you may see with a shy dog when you bring him to the greeting area is that he has the need to go to you for security. To me, this is almost always a good sign because the dog is *looking for that security.* In the first few weeks at home with your new dog, you will work hard on developing a relationship of trust with him. Most shyer dogs will seek out security, so if the dog quickly goes to you, and you reciprocate by giving the dog the security that he is asking for, it's a great way to start building your relationship for the future. Here are more tips for dealing with shy dogs:

Prey Drive

Before adopting a dog, you should understand what prey drive is and how to recognize it. Prey drive stems from the animal's instinctual desire to chase and kill other animals; a dog's breed or mix will affect the intensity of his prey drive. For example, Parson Russell Terriers were bred to catch vermin, and this can be seen today in the breed's propensity for chasing small critters. Prey drive can be triggered by various sights, sounds, and scents.

Take the opportunity to see what kind of prey drive a dog has when you meet him. If there are any toys in the greeting area, hold one up to see if the dog is interested in it. If the dog goes crazy for the toy and wants to hold it or chew on it, he most likely has a strong natural prey drive. If the dog tries to initiate a game of tug-of-war with you, this is another indication of prey drive.

If, among all of the distractions at the facility, including other dogs, people, unfamiliar smells, and noises, the dog still has an interest in the toy, his drive for it obviously supersedes his interest in the distractions around him. This most likely indicates a very high prey drive. I personally have a lot of fun with high-prey-drive dogs, but if you don't want a dog who's going to be very playful, with a desire to be mouthy, I suggest looking for a mellower dog.

- Sometimes your standing up can have an intimidating effect on a dog. Try to get down to the dog's level by simply kneeling. Sometimes a dog is more comfortable if he doesn't feel that you are towering over him.
- Don't reach for a shy dog; instead, let the dog come to you on his own terms.

Some high-strung dogs are very distracted by their surroundings while others want lots of interaction with their people.

HIGH-STRUNG DOGS

Your first meeting with a high-strung dog will give you a good idea about just how much energy he has. A high-strung dog can display various characteristics when you first meet him, such as high prey drive, jumping up on people, and being in constant motion.

The high-energy dog's body language will be much different from that of the shy dog. For example, the high-energy dog's ears will be perky. Keep in mind that there is a difference between the Golden Retriever–type (drop) ear and the German Shepherd–type (prick) ear. If a dog's ears are not standing straight up, don't mistake him for a shy dog. A drop-eared dog will hold his ears alert, so that the tops of the ears are about level with the top of the skull, when he is excited or interested in something.

A high-energy dog is likely to hold his tail up and wagging, but keep in mind that some dogs' tails are not designed to sit high above the back like a Shiba Inu's does. The tails of some dogs, such as Afghan Hounds, hang down. High-strung dogs will stand confidently, not hunched over.

While this dog may have a lot of self-confidence, there is a good possibility that his interest may not be in you. Do not let this lead you to believe that the dog does not like you, though. With all of the distractions in a shelter environment, it is very easy for a high-strung dog to become overwhelmed by everything around him.

If the dog is aloof and pacing at a distance from you, he is most likely a high-strung dog. Be patient and don't follow the dog around.

He may come to you on his own. If he doesn't, you should ask yourself if you have it in you to work with this dog to build a bond and train him, realizing that he may never become an affectionate, gregarious dog.

Remember, as with shy dogs, the characteristics of a high-strung dog can change. How long it takes really depends upon how energetic and easily distracted the dog is. Before adopting such a dog, you must ask yourself how much time, energy, and effort you are willing to put into giving this dog appropriate outlets for his energy and working with him so that he will bond with you and listen to you.

Caveats on Traits

Keep in mind that a dog does not have to display all of the traits mentioned to be considered a shy dog or a high-strung dog. For example, you may find a high-strung dog whose only body-language clue is his alert ear set. It also bears repeating that a dog's behavior and/or body language could be the result of his reactions to the shelter environment and meeting a new person—he may be uncomfortable or he may be overly excited.

Great Expectations

I think one of the mistakes potential adopters make when they first meet a new dog is that they set the bar too high. They expect too much too soon. A prospective dog owner might be looking for an instant connection—that magic moment—and it doesn't happen in the meet-and-greet area. It might take a few days or even a few weeks to really connect with the dog. Don't forget that although you are ready for a dog, the dog may not be ready for you.

The best advice I can give about your first meeting with a dog is to remember to go into it with a rational outlook. Understand that you do not know this dog and you likely know little to nothing about his history. Even more important is the fact that he does not know you, nor does he know your history. Just as our human relationships begin with a getting-to-know-you period, so do our relationships with our dogs. Coincidental? Not in the least. Read on.

2 getting ready

Before you go anywhere to start looking to adopt, you need to make certain that your home is ready and safe for a dog and that you have all of the supplies you'll need. As you are planning for a canine addition, think about the house in terms of two different areas: the inside and the outside. If you live in an apartment or townhouse, you likely will not have a yard to worry about, but you will still have to spend a significant amount of time outdoors, exercising your dog and giving him a chance to relieve himself.

Preparing Your Home Indoors

It takes some time for a dog to be allowed full run of the house with minimal supervision. Even when your dog has earned this privilege, you still want to ensure that he cannot get into places, such as kitchen and bathroom cabinets, where he could find trouble or danger. A dog could eat or drink something found in a cabinet that could make him very sick or worse. Keep cabinets tightly closed, and ask everyone else in the household to do the same. You may want to consider easy-to-install childproof locks on cabinets that contain food, household chemicals, cleaning products, and other off-limits items.

If everyone in the home puts everything back where it belongs and keeps their areas clean and neat, you will find it easier to have a harmonious relationship with your dog. If a dog you just adopted naturally likes to chew on things, he will pick up whatever he finds lying around, which can end up being both dangerous and destructive. For example, dogs love to chomp on dirty socks, which are soft and have an interesting odor—making them very appealing to a dog. But chewing indigestible material can be deadly for your dog, not to mention the damage to your belongings. The best way to prevent your dog from chewing on your belongings (or starting any bad habit) is to not give him the opportunity to do so in the first place. By keeping footwear and other "teeth-off" objects out of his reach, you're setting the dog up for success.

Another practice for your family to establish is keeping doors to the outside closed. There is a good chance that if your front or back door is open, the dog will dash through it. A well-trained dog will return when you call him, but it's likely that your new dog will *not* be trained to come when you call him, so don't give him the opportunity to bolt. Close doors promptly after entering or leaving, and keep them closed. Of course, no matter how many times you remind them, children and their friends are likely to forget and leave doors open, so you may want to crate the dog whenever you have guests and people are coming and going. (Crating will be discussed in more detail in Chapter 4.)

Before bringing the dog home, decide if there will be places in your home that are going to be off limits to him. If there is a certain room that your dog won't be allowed in, it is imperative that everyone understands that the door to that room must be shut at all times.

Keep a potential door-darter safe by closing doors and having the dog on his leash when people are coming and going.

It is also essential, before the dog comes home, that you choose part of a room that will be designated as his special area, the area in which he will stay when he is home alone. If your new four-legged friend is a puppy or a small dog, you can use a puppy pen that is tall enough to prevent him from getting out. The great thing about a puppy pen is that it is portable, allowing you to move it wherever you want fairly easily. Keep in mind, however, that eventually a puppy will learn how to escape from the pen as he grows, so you may want to consider getting a crate for safe confinement, too.

Preparing Your Home Outdoors

If you have a yard, it is of utmost importance to ensure that it is safe for your dog. You need to know that the fence is high enough and secure enough to prevent the dog from climbing or jumping over it

A safe fence is a sturdy one that the dog can't climb or jump over or dig under, with a gate that closes and locks securely.

or digging an escape tunnel underneath it. Check the entire perimeter of the fence. If the fence is made of wooden slats or boards, check that they are not broken, and make sure that no nails are sticking out for your dog to cut or scratch himself on.

Do you have gardeners or landscapers? Are you going to want your dog to be running around in the backyard when they are working? *My recommendation: keep the dog out of the yard when the gardeners come; when they leave, check that the gate is closed before you put the dog back in the yard.* I'd also make certain that no tools were left behind, as the dog could easily injure himself on them. If the dog does stay in the yard, the workers must know about his presence beforehand, and they must understand that they have to keep the gate closed. They have to be especially careful not to let the dog out when coming in and going out.

Finally, if you do not have a padlock on your gate, put one on immediately. Sadly, dogs are often stolen from backyards.

Supplies and Tools

Your house and yard are dog-proofed, but you also need to be ready for your new friend's arrival with the proper equipment. Make your preparations in advance, because you do not want to be running to the pet-supply store at the last minute. In the following sections, we'll discuss some of the items you will need.

BOWLS

You are going to need two bowls, one for water and one for food. You will see a wide variety of bowls at the pet-supply store. Stainless steel, plastic, and ceramic are popular materials, and they come in many different sizes. If you know the size of the dog you are adopting or looking

Bowl Caution

In the warmer months, make sure that stainless steel bowls are kept out of the sun. A stainless steel bowl left in the sun can get boiling hot, and if your dog's water is in it, the water will become too hot to drink. The sun does not stay in the same place throughout the day, so a bowl that was in the shade in the morning may be in the sun later in the day. Pay attention to stainless steel bowls kept outside, and move them as needed to make sure that they remain in the shade.

for, buy appropriately sized bowls—don't waste your money on bowls for a St. Bernard if you have your heart set on a dog the size of a Miniature Schnauzer. I am a huge fan of stainless steel bowls, and one of the reasons is that they are easy to clean.

FOOD

There is a huge variety of foods out there, and just like humans, dogs have different dietary needs. If you rescue a purebred dog, the rescuers may recommend a particular brand of food or a food with a specific ingredient because they believe that this is best for that breed. If the rescuer is a reputable breeder or someone else knowledgeable about the breed, I tend to take his or her advice to heart.

Be sure to take the time and read the ingredients of a food you're considering. For one thing, you want to find a quality protein source, such as chicken, lamb, or beef. Some foods will have a higher protein content than others, some foods use rice instead of corn and vice versa, some foods are all-natural or organic...if the variety of foods has you confused, ask a trusted source, such as your veterinarian.

If you have a puppy, remember that puppy food is made for a reason and that it contains ingredients that a growing dog needs during his first year.

COLLARS

For everyday use and for attaching the dog's ID tags, a regular nylon or leather buckle collar does the job. There are several types of training collars available, and they are only as good as the person on the

Switching Safely

Remember that if you switch your dog's food, you need to switch over to the new food gradually. A general rule of thumb is a ratio of three quarters old food to one quarter new food for the first two days; then, over the next two days, the dog's portion should be half old food and half new food. Follow with three quarters new food and one quarter old food for the next couple of days before offering a full portion of new food. If you change the food over too quickly, your dog could have diarrhea or stomach upset.

other end of the leash. They must be used correctly to be effective. When a chain choke collar is used properly, your dog will not feel discomfort. This type of collar is designed for giving the dog minimal corrections, just to get his attention. When you give the collar a small tug, it should release quickly; it is never used to restrain or pull the dog. Follow these steps to put a chain collar on your dog correctly:

1. **Stand facing your dog.**
2. **Hold the collar in your left hand so that it hangs down.**
3. **Take the bottom ring in your right hand.**
4. **Drop the chain into the bottom ring.**
5. **Turn the collar upside down and look for the letter P.**
6. **Place the collar over the dog's head.**

When put on the dog and used properly, the chain collar is a humane and effective training aid.

LEASHES

For an everyday leash, simple is best. I prefer a 6-foot-long leather leash, about 3/4 inch wide. Leather is a lot easier on the hands than cotton or nylon. You will use a long line in certain training exercises, such as teaching the dog to come; get one that is 30 feet long and made of a basic cotton web.

TOYS

A toy that I like for keeping a dog occupied is the hard rubber type with a hollow middle that you can fill with treats. Peanut butter works well, or you can even fill it with chicken broth and freeze it. These treats are good for your dog and will provide him with extended periods of playtime and keep him from chewing on inappropriate objects.

Toys run the gamut from those made of very hard rubber that is nearly impossible to chew through to plush, stuffed-animal-type squeaky toys. Your choice of toys will depend on your dog. Soft toys are fine for dogs who don't like to chew that much, but a high-prey-drive dog will tear one of these toys apart in seconds. You can run into problems if your dog ingests pieces of a toy, so strong chewers should only be given hard, durable toys.

CLEANING SUPPLIES

Setting your dog up for success in house-training is better than cleaning up after him, but you have to be prepared for the inevitable accidents. When it comes to cleaning supplies, simple is best. Keep white vinegar on hand to clean out your dog's crate. It is an odor neutral-

Don't underestimate small dogs when it comes to chewing, especially those breeds and mixes with vermin-catching in their background.

izer and is also very safe for the environment. To clean accidents from the carpet, try one of the stain removers made especially for cleaning up pet stains and odors. Eliminating odors is very important, because if a dog can smell a spot where he previously relieved himself, he will want to use that area as a bathroom again.

An appropriate toy for your dog will withstand his chewing and keep him occupied.

CRATE

Although crates are designed to be safe for transporting pets during travel, they have many uses in the home as well. A crate can serve as a safe retreat for your dog, as a place for him to sleep, and as a comfortable and secure place for him to stay when you're not home. A crate can also be used to help house-train your dog. (Using a crate for house-training is discussed in Chapter 4.)

Some crates are constructed of stiff metal wire, while others are made of sturdy, hard plastic. The type of crate you use is strictly up to you. The size of the crate, however, is one of the most important factors to consider when buying one.

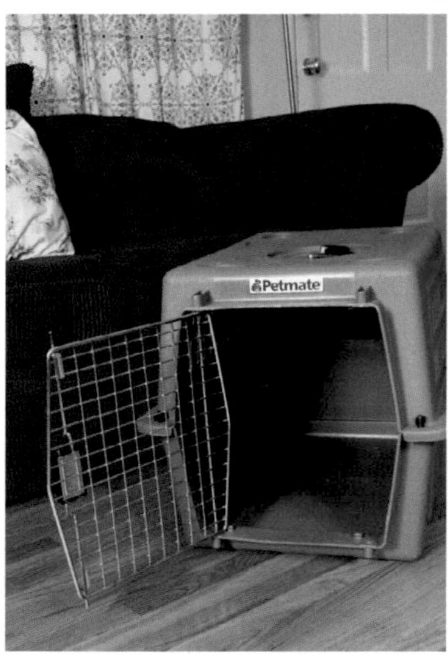

Your dog's crate should serve as a comfortable den.

A dog is a den animal, meaning that being in a *den*, or enclosed area, makes the animal feel comfortable and safe. If the crate is too big, it won't create a denlike environment; the dog also will be able to relieve himself in the crate if he has too much room in it. If it's too small, it will not be fair to the animal. You want to choose a crate that your dog can stand up in without touching the top and that he can turn around in comfortably.

Other Members of the Household

There are two other important factors to think about regarding the environment into which you'll be bringing the new dog: other pets in the home and children. Some dogs may have already formed attitudes about other animals and kids based on past experiences, while others were "only pets" or lived in kid-free homes. I've put together a few points for you to think about before adopting.

EXISTING PETS

If you already have a dog (or dogs) in your home, you want to first make sure, before you adopt another one, that your resident dog gets along with others of his kind. Most dogs do, but just as some people do not like other people, some dogs simply do not like other dogs.

Once you've determined that your present dog will be OK with a new canine addition to the family, consider the sex of the dog you are going to adopt. Remember that, as a general rule of thumb, most males get along better with females and most females get along better with males. Having two dogs of the same sex will not necessarily create a problem; however, there is a better chance that they will get along if they are of the opposite sex. I address in Chapter 7 how to properly introduce your new dog to your current dog and how to socialize them.

If you have a cat who has previously shown a dislike or fear of dogs, you need to consider if adopting a dog is the right thing to do in fairness to both animals. However, many cats and dogs do tolerate each other's presence. Your resident cat may not have a fondness for a new dog coming into the home, but the two could coexist peacefully. (We also talk in Chapter 7 about socializing dogs with cats).

With some socialization, most dogs can learn to see eye-to-eye.

If you have a bird that you keep in a cage, make sure that the bird's cage is in a place that will be safe. A dog with a high prey drive might scare the bird or possibly do something worse if he can get close enough to the cage. The same goes for small mammals, such as hamsters, gerbils, and guinea pigs.

CHILDREN

If you have children, one of the most important variables to consider is their ages. If your child is two years old or younger, ask yourself if you are really going to have the time for your child and a new dog. Like a baby, a new dog needs lots of love and attention, supervision, guidance, and interaction with you. A new dog also needs time for training and exercise. Consider honestly whether you have the time and energy for everything that a dog needs, as you do not want to adopt a dog into a less-than-ideal situation. Keep in mind that you don't have to forgo adoption forever; just wait until your child is older and you have the time for a new four-legged family member.

If you have a toddler and think you can handle both a toddler and a new dog, then think about the size of the dog that you want to adopt. A large, active dog—puppy or adult— can be a hazard around your child. He could knock down the child or hit him or her in the face with a furiously wagging tail. If the new adoptee is a puppy,

A well-behaved child can be a dog's favorite playmate.

it is imperative that small children understand how to handle him. Without the proper supervision, a puppy can be squeezed too tightly or even dropped and injured. Supervision and instruction on how to properly handle a dog of any size must come from you.

If your kids are a little older, you need to set down some guidelines and rules before the new dog comes home. They need to be aware of making sure that the doors with outside access are kept closed, that outside gates are kept locked, and that personal possessions are not left around the house for the dog to start chewing on. Any of your children's friends who visit the house must also be aware of the rules. If you are going to assign some of the doggie-care tasks to an older child, discuss these responsibilities before bringing the dog home so that the child knows what is expected of him or her.

Plan Your Adoption Day

The best thing that you can do when adopting your dog is to plan out several days for home preparation, bringing your dog home, and allowing him to adjust to you and the new situation. An adjustment period, during which you can be home with the dog, is especially important if the dog eventually will be left alone during the day. It's rare that you will walk into a shelter and go home with a dog on the same day. Often, whether you adopt from a shelter, humane society, or rescue organization, you will fill out an application, meet the dog, perhaps have a home visit from adoption volunteers, and wait while you are approved for adoption. Once approved, you can make arrangements for bringing the dog home. Here are some suggestions for people who work full-time weekdays outside of the home:

- **Bring the dog home on a Wednesday evening or early in the day on Thursday and take Thursday and Friday off; that would give you four days to be home with your new dog.**
- **Leave work early on a Friday, pick up the dog, and take him home with you; that will give you almost three days.**
- **If you cannot take off any time during the week, plan to bring the dog home on Friday evening or Saturday morning and spend the entire weekend with him.**

Whatever your work schedule is, just try to give yourself as many days as possible to spend with the dog after the adoption day. The next few chapters will go into much more detail.

Your adopted dog's homecoming is an exciting time and the start of a beautiful new relationship.

3 the first two hours at home

This chapter, albeit brief, was really the main reason for my writing this book. The first two hours at home with your new dog are critical to laying a good foundation for future success. Not properly introducing your dog to his new home is something that can have both an immediate impact and, more importantly, a long-term effect on the dog. I want you to understand what you need to do when you first bring your dog home and give you a game plan for doing it.

The First Thirty Minutes

In your first thirty minutes at home with your dog, you need to think about two things: making the dog as comfortable as possible and taking the opportunity to learn about him.

THE FIRST TEN MINUTES

When you first bring the dog home, take him directly into your backyard on leash. Be sure to securely close and lock the gate behind you. Once you and the dog are safely enclosed in the yard, remove the leash and let the dog wander. There are many new smells and new things for your dog to see, and sometimes it's best to just let him explore. One of the mistakes new owners might make is to follow the dog around the yard, hovering over him. Many times, kids will follow the dog around, and I do not think that's the best thing to do at this point. Just let the dog sniff around, and give him the opportunity to eliminate. Don't give in to the urge of trying to call the dog to you.

Whether off leash in the backyard or on leash around the neighborhood, there will be a feast of sights, smells, and sounds for your new dog.

I think that during the first ten minutes, it is best to just let the dog do his own thing.

If you live in an apartment or townhouse and do not have a yard, the first thing you should do is take the dog for a walk to allow him to relieve himself and get acquainted with the sights and smells of the neighborhood.

The great part about this first ten minutes is that the dog will probably be relieving himself outside as he's roaming around the yard or walking with you. Remember that house-training is a behavior that begins outside, and this is part of that training process. If the dog defecates in the backyard, don't pick the feces up immediately. You are trying to condition the dog to urinate and defecate outside, so you want the dog to remember his "bathroom" area the next time he goes outside. If the feces is left there, the dog will get the idea that he should continue going in that place. After a few days, you can pick it up; from then on, clean up the yard every day.

Dog-to-Dog Introductions

Steps for introducing your new dog to your resident dog are given in Chapter 7, but if you'd like your new dog to meet a friend's or neighbor's dog after he's had some time to acclimate, do so in neutral territory, not in the other dog's yard. For example, you can meet the person and dog at a local park. This should not be a dog park, however, as there are too many variables that you cannot control, and you don't want to have an incident with your new dog on his first day with you.

If you live in an apartment or townhouse, look for patterns in the places where your dog might want to urinate or defecate on his walks. Be sure to always to pick up after your dog immediately.

Remember that dogs are naturally social, and many of them love to simply be petted. Any opportunity you have to kneel down and pet the dog is huge. This builds the relationship between you and your dog and gives shyer dogs the security that they crave.

During this first ten minutes, you will start to see the dog's true personality emerge. For that to happen, you must allow the dog do what he naturally wants to do. Everyone should lay low and let the dog hang out on his own. If your dog is sniffing around the backyard

After ten minutes of exploring his surroundings outdoors, it's time for the dog to come in and see his new home.

and wants to stop and come to you, that's great, but remember that the new smells are going to be a lot more interesting to him than you are at this point.

As you are watching your dog, ask yourself the following:

- **Are there objects, sounds, or other animals on which he is fixating?**
- **Do cars and other moving objects easily distract him?**
- **Is he is pacing quickly, or is he walking around casually, enjoying the sights and smells?**
- **Does he appear to be shy or timid?**

The more prey drive a dog has, the more he will fixate on things such as squirrels or birds in the yard and adjacent areas. More prey-driven dogs will also move a little faster, while mellow dogs and timid dogs will move more slowly.

THE SECOND TEN MINUTES

It is now time to bring the dog into the apartment, house, or townhouse. Up to this point, your dog has been either exploring the backyard on leash or on an on-leash walk with you. We'll assume that the dog has urinated and possibly defecated during the first ten minutes.

A common mistake that many owners make when they go inside is to *unhook the leash and let the dog loose.* If you let your dog loose in the house, he is most likely going to go into places you don't want him to be. The dog doesn't know the difference! If given free rein right off the bat, he will think it's OK to wander around the house wherever he wants, jump up on the couch, rummage through the trash cans, and put his feet up on the kitchen counter. And why wouldn't he? He has not been shown that these actions are wrong. The best way to deal with all unwanted behaviors is to make sure that they never have the opportunity to happen in the first place.

Here is my suggestion: attach the leash to your dog's collar when you are outside if he has been off leash in the yard. Take your dog into the house on leash so that you have total control. You are not going to have to constantly call your dog and tell him "No" if you have him on leash and can control what he does. If you want to hang out in the living room and watch some TV, just take the dog with you. If you need to go into the bedroom to get something, just take the dog with you.

Keep your dog on leash and let him do what makes him comfortable.

With the right type of introductions from the beginning, children and dogs can be the best of friends.

If you have a family, this is a great time to let the dog really meet everyone. A suggestion is to let the dog go to each person, instead of everyone coming to the dog. Just walk him on his leash up to each person in whom he's interested. I know that kids can get very excited about the new dog coming home, but sometimes if they follow the dog around and do not give him enough space, it can give the dog a negative association with the children right off the bat. It is really up to the adults to relay this information to the children.

Something else you may want to do is to offer the dog a few treats. If the dog takes the treats, it will make this first ten minutes inside his new home an even more positive experience. Limit the amount of treats to just a few, but each family member should have the chance to give the dog a treat and spend a few moments with him.

THE LAST TEN MINUTES

The following ten minutes will involve your taking the dog outside again. If you have a fenced yard, you'll take him out into the yard, secure the gate, and remove his leash. If you don't have a fenced yard, you'll take him out, on leash, to a nearby grassy area or for a walk around the block. This will give the dog another opportunity to relieve himself, as well as give you a chance to see if there's a bit of a change in your dog from when you were outside earlier. Does he seem a little less distracted? Does he seem a little more comfortable? Did he urinate or defecate right away? If your dog appears to be a less distracted and more interested in you, now is a good time to engage him in some play.

If you have a yard, take a few toys and balls outside with you. If you're in an apartment, take the dog back inside as soon as he's relieved himself and clear a safe space to play with your dog. Pay attention to how the dog responds to the toys; his response can give you important information about his personality. For instance, dogs

In the course of having fun with your dog, you can find out valuable information about his personality, prey drive, and activity level.

with higher prey drive are more likely to be interested in toys right away than dogs with little or no prey drive.

Playtime should be on the dog's terms. For example, if you throw a ball and the dog does not return it to you, don't worry about it. You simply want to be doing things that make the dog happy.

If you have a more timid dog, and he seems shy or nervous, keep an eye out for things that could be making him uncomfortable. It might be something you cannot see or smell, but you'll be able to tell by his body language that something is affecting him. If he's acting nervous, remove him from the area.

Instead of starting to train your dog, use this first thirty-minute phase as a time of observation and learning for you and your dog. No matter his personality, you are going to want to take every opportunity you can in the first half hour at home to really *get to know and understand* your dog.

The Next Thirty Minutes

So you have just completed the first half hour of your first two hours with your new dog. As you and your dog were outside again during the last ten minutes, we'll assume that your dog took care of his business during that time.

We are now going to take the dog inside again on leash. You might feel that if the dog was good in the house when you brought him inside the first time, you can now take the leash off. I highly recommend that you keep the leash on while the dog is indoors during the first two-hour period. One of the reasons for this is that you want to avoid correcting the dog. Remember, it is totally natural for a dog to want to wander around, investigate, and maybe pick things up in his mouth. What an owner often ends up doing is following the dog around the house, saying "Don't go in there," "Get off there," "Stay out of there," and "No." However, you want to save these things for times when you actually *need* to correct the dog. In training exercises discussed later in the book, we use the word "No." But during the dog's first twenty-four hours at home, let's try to keep everything as positive as possible. This starts with preventing the dog from roaming freely around the house.

Once back indoors, let your dog go about your business with you as you keep him close by.

During this second thirty-minute interval, do whatever you'd normally do while keeping the dog on the leash. Whatever you do—be it watch TV, go on the computer, or talk on the telephone—it is essential that you are aware of your dog and that you are doing whatever comes naturally, such as petting him, in your interactions with him. If he starts to fidget or look uncomfortable, he may need to relieve himself again. Since he's already on leash, you can quickly whisk him outside for a potty trip and immediately bring him back indoors after he's done what he needs to do.

The dog is going to have a few choices during this thirty-minute period. He may stand there—although he is not likely to stand for the entire half hour—or he may sit or lie down. It may take him some time to calm down, but eventually he will do one of those three things.

During this time, more laid-back dogs and shyer dogs are the ones who are most likely to either sit or lie down. A timid dog may want to

It's a good sign if your dog looks to you for security and wants to be close to you.

lie down close to you or sit in your lap. If the dog needs the security of being close to you, make sure he is as comfortable as possible. This type of contact is a great way to start building trust with a shy or timid dog.

With a more confident, active dog, you may find him wanting to pace around a bit, but the great part about having the dog on leash is that he cannot go anywhere. It may take some resolve on your part for first ten to fifteen minutes to just stay in place and let the dog settle down. You may see the dog sitting for a minute and then getting up. The dog may just stand there for a few minutes and then start pacing a little. The dog may lie down for a few minutes and then get up again. Higher-energy dogs will likely want to move around more than mellower dogs do.

During this period, all we are doing is beginning the conditioning stage. We are conditioning the dog to live our lifestyle, and this will be more difficult in the beginning.

Hour Two

Dedicate the second hour of your time at home with your new dog to more playtime, followed by a nice walk for exercise. You can use this playtime to find out some of the things that the dog likes. Start off with balls and toys. If you are dealing with a high-energy dog, you will find that he most likely will be into playing with a variety of toys, and you can see if there are certain toys that he likes better than others. This is not to say that timid or mellower dogs will not be eager to play with toys, but dogs with higher prey drive, as we've already discussed, are more likely to really be interested in toys. An extremely active dog with a high prey drive is most likely to be "toy crazy," as some trainers call it.

What if your dog doesn't want to play with a toy? There are some dogs who have very little prey drive or who have absolutely no interest in toys. Treats are a good alternative for a dog who does not like to play with toys because it gives you a chance to interact with him and give him something that he likes. Because something good is coming from you, it helps the dog build a positive connection to you.

Even if your dog likes to play with toys, also try giving your dog some different types of treats. I have used Bil-Jac treats for a number of years, and they come in a variety in sizes and flavors. Quite often, treats that are soft and easy to chew are easier and more palatable for some dogs.

Let the dog's mood and energy level dictate what you do during playtime. Even high-energy dogs need a break sometimes!

It's never too early to build a connection with your new dog, and following a plan for the first two hours at home allows you to do just that.

End this hour with a nice long walk. Exercise is great for all dogs, but it is essential for higher-energy dogs, who both want and need to move. If, for some reason, your dog resists taking a walk, I recommend that you bring a few treats with you so you can encourage him to walk along with you and reward him as he does. This will reinforce proper leash manners because you want him to walk by your side and at your pace, while giving the dog exercise and showing him that on-leash walks are enjoyable.

When you look back at the last two hours, you'll see that you've been able to give your dog ample opportunity to relieve himself outside, along with a good amount of exercise. He has started to learn how to be a good member of the family just by hanging out with you as you went about some of your everyday activities. Over the next few days, as you start to feel a little more comfortable with your dog around the house, you can start taking his leash off for short periods of time. Slowly increase the amount of your dog's off-leash time each day until he is no longer on leash in the house.

An on-leash walk provides the dog with many things: exercise, a chance to relieve himself, time to learn about his new surroundings, and, most importantly, quality time to bond with you.

4 house-training

A dog's relieving himself in the house is probably the most common behavior issue that owners must deal with. This can happen within the first few minutes of bringing the new dog home and is likely the result of the dog's not knowing any better and the owner's not having control over the situation. I have seen house-training problems begin very slowly and become major over time. What starts as a few potty "accidents" in the house can turn into a full-blown problem before the owner knows it.

In most cases that I've seen, house-training problems stem from the owner's giving the dog the opportunity to roam freely in the house when the animal is first brought home. If you let almost any new dog run around the house unsupervised, the dog is more than likely going to have an accident. If you remember from our discussion of the first two hours at home in Chapter 3, we never gave the dog the opportunity to relieve himself indoors because we kept him on leash at all times, we were constantly with him, and we got him outside right away at any sign of his needing to "go."

Your new dog may have been house-trained in his previous home. If he has, good for you! He already has the basic idea of relieving himself outdoors, which means that you're a step ahead. However, you will still need to train him to his new home and schedule and give him time to adjust. If he has not been house-trained, then obviously you'll be starting from scratch. Either way, your first step is to set up a plan of attack and decide what training technique

Avoid giving your dog free run of the house until he is completely house-trained and you can trust him around your belongings.

you are going to use. For the sake of this discussion, we'll assume that the dog is not house-trained (you can adjust your approach depending on your dog).

There are two approaches to house-training: preventative training and corrections. *Preventative training* means that you don't give the animal a chance to start developing a bad behavior. With preventative training, we *never* put the dog in an area where he is unsupervised and has the chance to develop bad potty behavior. In dealing with this specific behavior, you are going to use a preventative-training technique called *crate-training.*

Crate-training is one of the most important preventative-training techniques. It is also an effective method for eliminating a problem behavior that has already developed, specifically potty problems. The best thing about crate-training is that it *never* gives the dog the opportunity to be in a problem area unsupervised.

Using *corrections* means letting a dog know when he does something that you don't want him to do. You might find yourself correcting your dog if he relieves himself in the house, but unless you catch him in the act, this will not be very effective. The ideal correction is based on perfect timing. You will want to say "No" when the dog is either starting to lift his leg or beginning to urinate or defecate. We will discuss corrections more in Chapter 8. In this chapter, we'll focus on crate-training.

Understanding Your Dog and House-training

Let me repeat—the biggest mistake a new dog owner can make is to let the dog wander from room to room unsupervised. Think about it from your dog's point of view: if he hasn't been house-trained, and you are not right there to instruct him, he does not know that relieving himself inside is different from relieving himself outside, so why would he *not* relieve himself in the house? He has never been taught what to do or what not to do. Like a child, an animal needs direction; this is especially true if you're dealing with a puppy. Countless pet owners have told me: "I don't understand it. I brought my dog home and let him loose, and he immediately lifted his leg on my couch." *How can we just assume that a dog automatically knows that this behavior is wrong?* A further problem is that when an animal is brought into a new home and relieves himself indoors, he will most often repeat the mistake in the same spot.

House-training, despite its name, is a behavior that begins outside. This is why I advised you to spend most of your first thirty minutes at home outside with the dog (see Chapter 3). By doing so, you give your dog every opportunity to start becoming conditioned to relieving himself outdoors as well as to start getting to know his new living area. You must be outside with him and *actually see him* relieve himself. Don't put your dog in the backyard and walk away for a few minutes. If he didn't relieve himself outside, and you bring him back into the house, there is a good possibility that he will relieve himself indoors. *Make sure that he "goes"!*

If your dog is already having potty-training problems, look at where the accidents are happening. Is the dog relieving himself in the living room or dining room only? Maybe it's happening all over the entire house. If your dog is urinating or defecating anywhere in your house, here are some points to think about:

- **The only way for house-training to work is for everyone in the household to be consistent with the dog. This means that everyone must know where the dog is having accidents, and everyone must be doing the same things to try to extinguish the behavior.**
- **You cannot allow the dog to be in the problem areas unsupervised at any time. If he is, he will have an accident.**

How do you accomplish this, especially if the dog is having accidents all over the house? The solution is crate-training, and it has worked for countless dog owners.

Crate-training Technique

Crate-training is one of the simplest, easiest, and most common training techniques for owner and dog. It is also one of the best preventative-training techniques. Dog trainers will disagree on many issues, but it's hard to find a trainer who doesn't agree that crate-

Training a dog to use a specific potty area is quite natural, as a dog will sniff out where he's gone before and use that area again.

training is a great way to prevent or get rid of many behavior problems, especially house-training problems.

As I've mentioned, most dogs will not develop bad behaviors if they are not given the opportunity to let them begin, and this is the very premise on which crate training is based. In general, most dogs will not eliminate in areas where he sleeps, so the crate is designed to take the place of the animal's den.

There are many different types of crates: the hard plastic ones, such as the type used for travel, work well for crate-training. Wire crates and pens can work for crate-training, too, but because they are much more open, they don't re-create the den atmosphere as much. Nonetheless, these types of crates do give the dog a place of his own and are typically preferred for larger dogs. Whatever type of crate or pen you choose, it will be a place where the animal can stay safely for periods of time when you do not want him wandering the house unsupervised. Here are the basic principles of crate-training:

- **Dogs will not eliminate in their sleeping areas. Accustom your dog to spending time in his crate so he is comfortable in it and thinks of it as his den.**

A hard-sided plastic crate re-creates a cozy den environment for the dog.

- Once your dog is accustomed to the crate, he need never be left loose and unsupervised, which in turn means he will never get the opportunity to relieve himself in the house. He will either be resting in his crate or spending time out of the crate with a family member who can get him outside as soon as he shows any indication of needing to relieve himself.
- With diligence, consistency, and patience, you can prevent house-training problems from happening or eventually extinguish any potty problem your dog already had.

Crate-training Game Plan

Now that you know the basic idea behind crate-training as a house-training method, let me tell you how to accustom your dog to the crate so that he is comfortable with it. (Whether you are using a crate or a pen, from this point on, I will refer to it as a *crate.*) An excellent way to start doing this is to feed him in his crate, leaving the crate door open. By offering food in the crate and allowing the dog to go in and out of the crate as he pleases, you're helping the dog create a positive connection with the crate.

A wire crate is more open but also serves as a suitable den.

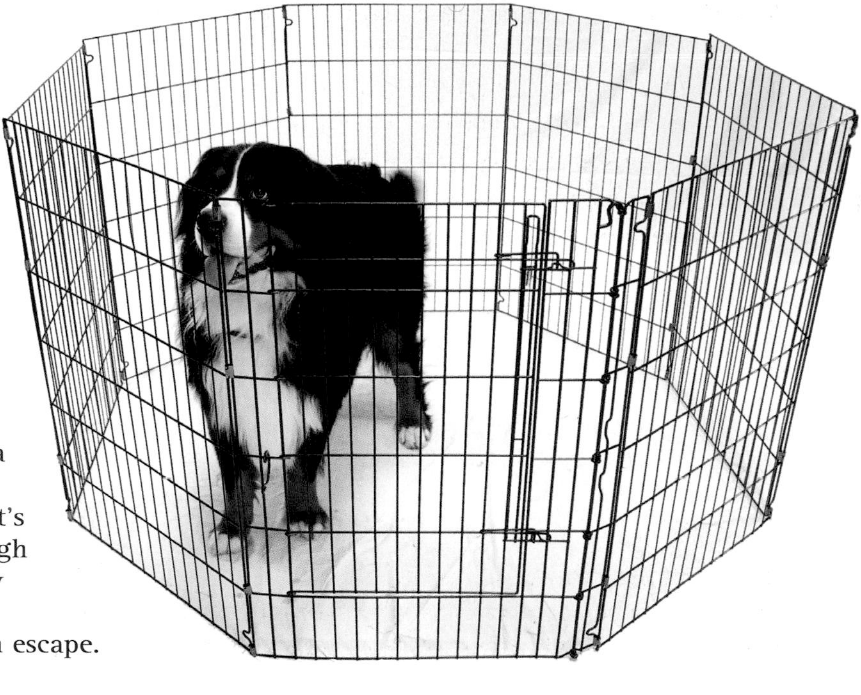

Next, put some other things that the dog likes, such as treats and toys, inside the crate. These will help as you're beginning to train him to spend time in the crate. You can even designate a specific type of treat—something that your dog especially likes—for crate time only.

When choosing a pen, make sure that it's high enough and sturdy enough to prevent an escape.

Here is a step-by-step game plan for accustoming the dog to his crate over the period of two to seven days:

1. Scatter six or seven broken-up treats in the back of the crate. This way, the dog has to go all the way into the crate. *It is essential that the dog knows that he can eat the treats and come out of the crate as he chooses.* Make this a very short training session—simply repeat the sequence of the dog's going into the crate, eating the treats, and coming out of the crate a few times. Repeat this short training session several times throughout the day.

2. After the third or fourth such training session, shut the crate door for about ten seconds when the dog goes into the crate to eat the treats. After ten seconds, open the door and let the dog come out. *The dog must not feel like he is trapped.*

3. Repeat the sequence again, but this time leave the crate door open so that the dog can eat the treats and exit the crate when he wants to do so. The purpose here is to remain unpredictable. The dog never knows if you are going to shut the door or leave it open.

4. The next time the dog goes into the crate, shut the door for thirty seconds and then let him out.

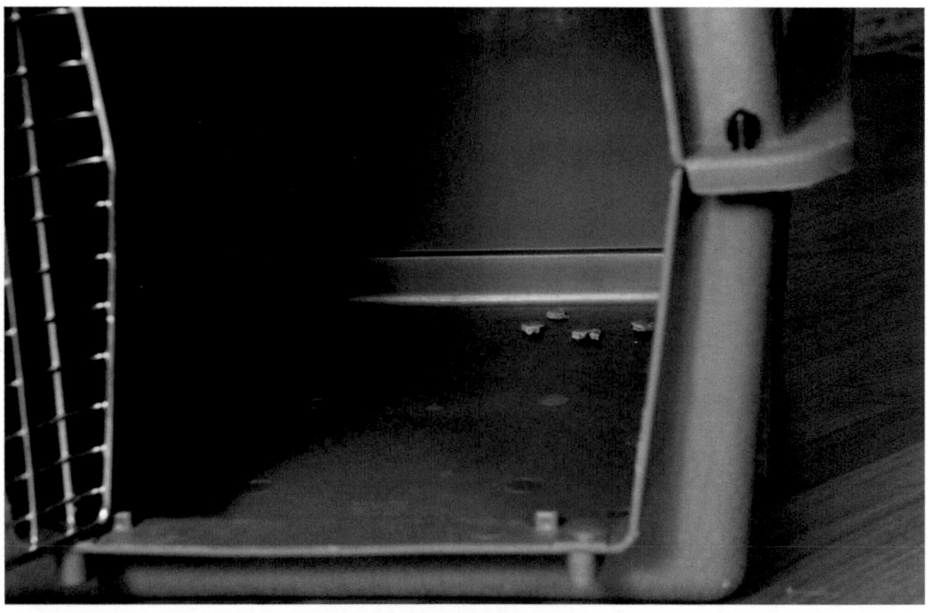

Place the broken-up treats at the back of the crate and encourage the dog to walk into the crate to get them.

Going into the crate and getting a tasty reward should convince the dog right off the bat that the crate is a pleasant place to be.

5. Close the crate door when the dog goes in, and then walk into another room for about a minute. Your dog will most likely not make any noise, but if he does bark or whine, do absolutely nothing. Wait for about a minute, or until the dog is quiet, and then return to open the crate door and let him out. It's important that you do not let the dog out when he is barking or whining; if you do, he will think all he has to do to get out is complain!

6. Repeat the previous step, but this time leave the dog in the crate for about five minutes. If your dog is barking or whining initially, don't worry; you'll find that he will whine or bark less over time as he learns that only when he's quiet will you let him out.

7. Half an hour later, repeat the previous step three times, but increase the dog's time in the crate to ten to fifteen minutes. One of the three times, however, switch things up by putting the dog in the crate, shutting the door, opening the door about *five seconds*

While You're Sleeping

Once your dog is house-trained, if you let him sleep loose in your room, keep the crate in your room with the crate door open to give him the option of going into the crate to sleep.

I also recommend that, until your dog is thoroughly trained, you keep the door to your room shut so he is completely confined there and cannot roam around the house and have an accident. After at least a week with no accidents overnight, you can open your bedroom door at night to give your dog free run of the house, if you wish.

later, and putting the leash on the dog to take him outside. Remain unpredictable so the dog never knows how long he will be in the crate. We want to send a message that it may be as little as five seconds or as long as a couple of hours.

8. Take a half-hour break, and then repeat the previous step, this time increasing the time in the crate to twenty to thirty minutes. As you did previously, mix things up one time by letting the dog out after five seconds, putting his leash on him, and taking him outside.

9. Over the next few days, you can start increasing your dog's crate time to about an hour each session. Again, once each day, put the dog into the crate, shut the door, open it about five seconds later, put the leash on the dog, and take him outside.

Put the crate in your bedroom, at least during the night, so the dog will be sleeping next to you and can alert you if he needs to go out. This way, you can ensure that there will be no accidents at night. When you wake up each morning, the first thing you should do is open the crate, put a leash on the dog, and take him outside.

You can see how these small steps will condition your dog to staying in his crate and "holding it" until you let him outside. The most important aspect of house-training is paying attention to your dog. It won't take him long to associate going outside with relieving himself, so he'll start letting you know when he wants to go outside. Scratching at the door, barking, or just spending time near the window or door are good indications that he needs to go outside.

Help your dog achieve house-training success by paying attention to his body language and being ready to take him outside when duty calls.

5 understanding "what color is your dog?"

First, let me thank every one of the clever dog owners who have attended my seminars, especially the ones who've answered my opening question with a loud, bold "White!", "Black!", or "Brown!" "Yellow" for a Labrador Retriever could have started a good conversation about my color system, but white, black, and brown simply don't make the list. The color system that I refer to is not about the color of a dog's coat, but rather his personality and temperament. From the hot-under-the-collar Red dog to the shrinking-violet Blue dog, every dog can be described by one of my five colors.

Knowing his "color" will help you determine the best way to train your dog, as his personality and temperament offer clues about how he will learn most effectively. This color-coding system will not only help you train your dog but also help you get to know him better.

In my first book, "*What Color Is Your Dog?*", I addressed two points that I don't feel most dog trainers emphasize enough: the importance of building a bond with a new puppy or dog and the simple fact that all dogs are different, even purebred dogs from the same litter.

HOSPITAL

The Dog–Owner Bond

To have success when training your dog, you must develop a relationship with him so that he is eager to please you. A dog who likes you and trusts you is far more likely to obey you. Any successful dog trainer will tell you that when your dog wants to please you and make you happy, training is 100 percent easier. The mistake that so many new owners make is immediately assuming the "top dog" or alpha role, ordering the dog around like a drill sergeant would. Instead, it's far better to spend the first few weeks getting to know your dog and building a lifelong bond of trust and loyalty than trying to master the *sit, stay, and down* cues on your dog's first day home.

A bond of affection and trust lays a positive foundation for everything you do with your dog, and its importance cannot be overemphasized.

High prey drive and love of the chase—which often goes hand in hand with pulling on the leash—are common traits of high-strung dogs.

Different Dogs, Different Colors

All dogs are different, and this is something that I emphasize to all new owners. Things that work well for one dog may not work well for another. We all know that people are unique and have different personalities, and this also holds true for dogs. Even in a litter of purebred puppies, you will find that each puppy has a different temperament and personality type—some will be shy and withdrawn, some will be mellow and easygoing, and some will be active and assertive.

Some high-strung dogs are easily distracted while others are gregarious and demonstrative.

According to my system, there are five different color categories for dogs—Red, Orange, Yellow, Green, and Blue—based on their personalities. I define a Red dog as one whose energy level is off the charts and whose attention moves from one thing to the next as quickly as the squirrel he's likely to be chasing. An Orange dog is less wild but is still high-strung and fairly difficult to control. A Yellow dog is the ideal—this is a middle-of-the-road, mellow dog and is by far the easiest type of dog to train and to live with. A Green dog tends to be timid and a bit insecure, and a Blue dog is overly fearful and nervous. Both Green and Blue dogs are challenging to train and require plenty of positive reinforcement and bolstering to encourage them.

How do you determine your dog's color? Although most owners wish that their dogs were essentially Yellow, the majority of untrained dogs fall to the left (Red or Orange) or right (Green or Blue) of the color spectrum. It's always easy to recognize the extremes, whether a dog is bouncing off the wall or is skittish and retiring. There are some things that will help you determine your dog's specific color.

A cooler-colored dog displays his shyness through body language such as hunching over, avoiding eye contact, and hesitating to approach you.

If your dog is high-strung to any degree, ask yourself the following questions:

- **How high-strung is my dog?**
- **Does he constantly jump on people?**
- **Does he bark wildly and act out of control when you come home?**
- **Does he pull hard on the leash when I walk him?**
- **Does he display a little aggression from time to time, or is he a complete bully?**
- **Does my dog live to chase squirrels, toddlers, bikes, and anything else that moves?**
- **Does my dog chew up everything in his path, from socks to furniture legs to my wagging fingers?**
- **Does my dog fixate on things, such as squirrels and birds in the backyard?**
- **Does my dog exhibit prey drive? If so, how intense is that drive?**

Reassure a shy dog by doing things like moving slowly, talking gently, getting down to his level, and letting him sniff your hand.

If your dog is quite high-strung, has most or all of these characteristics, and displays these traits more often than not, he is most likely a Red dog. If your dog displays most of these characteristics at more moderate levels, he is most likely an Orange dog. As your dog progresses with his training, he will usually not remain a Red or Orange dog. A major goal in my system is to get your dog moving toward the center of the color spectrum to become a "mellow Yellow."

The Warm-colored Dogs

You're sure you have an energetic dog, meaning that he is one of the warmer-colored dogs, either Orange or Red. Here's a quick list of characteristics to help you figure out his exact color.

Orange

- Puts feet up on people
- Is very excitable
- Pulls moderately on leash
- Is a little too playful

Red

- Is overly jumpy
- Pulls hard on leash
- Does not stay in one place
- Has a short attention span
- Is overly playful

Extremely Red

- Is hyperactive
- Jumps up uncontrollably
- Is very mouthy
- Pulls very hard on the leash

For dogs on the other end of the spectrum, the shy or timid dogs, ask yourself these questions:

- **Is my dog afraid of people he doesn't know?**
- **Is my dog afraid of other dogs or the family cat?**
- **Does he get nervous when I correct him or even when I just say "No"?**
- **Does my dog try to run away?**
- **Is he naturally nervous? Does he shake sometimes?**

If your dog has most or all of these characteristics and displays them often, he is most likely a Blue dog. If your dog displays some of these characteristics, but not to the extremes that a Blue dog does, then he is most likely a Green dog.

The Cool-colored Dogs

You're sure you have a shy, cool-colored (Green or Blue) dog, but you're not sure of his exact color. Here's a quick list of characteristics to help you decide.

Green	Blue	Extremely Blue
• Is somewhat cautious • Is reserved • Is slightly timid and coy • Likes most people	• Is slightly nervous • Is afraid of certain people • Is a little jumpy • Holds tail between legs • Shakes sometimes	• Shakes uncontrollably • Tucks tail between legs constantly • Is afraid of most people • Is extremely worried and edgy

The same concept applies to this side of the color spectrum. As your dog progresses with his training, he will usually move toward the center of the spectrum, closer to being a Yellow dog.

If you've gone through all of the aforementioned questions and have shaken your head "No" to most, if not all, of them, congratulations! You may have been lucky enough to have adopted a Yellow dog! Training a Yellow dog is straightforward and shouldn't be too challenging, yet it will be just as rewarding as training any other color of dog.

The Yellow dog has a naturally laid-back personality. This dog, right in the middle of the color spectrum, lacks the extreme characteristics found on the outer edges of the color spectrum. You will find that the Yellow dog's attitude will quite often be dictated by you, the owner. Think about the people you know who are very easygoing. Quite often, they just kind of *go with the flow.* If you're happy

A "mellow Yellow" dog is at ease with the world around him and feels comfortable almost anywhere.

and excited, so is this type of person; if you're more low-key, so is he. The same thing applies to the Yellow dog. If you're firm and in control of your voice and mannerisms, the dog will be calm. If you are animated and excited, the dog's excitement level will increase. This can play a very important role in training because your demeanor affects your dog's responses.

Because of their distance from the center of the spectrum, the Red and Blue dogs are going to need the most patience. If you take a look at the personalities of Red and Blue dogs, you'll see that they could not be more different, and that is exactly why they are on opposite ends of the color spectrum. So if the dogs themselves are total opposites, it makes sense that the way you talk to, touch, and act around these dogs, as well as the techniques you use to train them, would also be totally different. Each color requires its own approach to bonding, socialization, and training, which you will see in later chapters as we discuss problem-solving and teaching cues.

Walks are much more fun with a dog who behaves on lead, not lunging, pulling, or trying to take off after small critters.

the first thirty days

My first dog, Shadow, acquired her name quickly. An extremely timid terrier cross, she followed me constantly from the day she was dropped off at our house. I was just thirteen years old, and she was a tiny puppy. Shadow simply could not stop shaking and was so nervous and shy that it was no wonder she was the last puppy left in her litter. Training a dog like Shadow would be a challenge for an experienced dog trainer, so you can imagine what it was like for a thirteen-year-old whose knowledge of dogs covered TV, movie, and comic-strip characters. Shadow was no Lassie or Snoopy!

With no dog experience—much less any training experience—I simply did everything I could think of to make Shadow's days nothing but positive. We spent time doing things together, and I searched hard to find activities and objects that she liked.

In truth, Shadow wasn't the best-looking puppy or even that much fun—she basically didn't like toys or treats, which really spells "killjoy" in dogspeak. She did, however, like to follow me around, so that's what

Shadow, pictured here, and the author learned from each other.

we did. I based our entire relationship on "follow the leader."

At first, there really was very little I could teach her. Shadow was not the kind of dog who would respond to "firm but fair" cues. What I could teach her was that I was a friend and she could trust me.

The more time Shadow and I spent together, the stronger her bond with me grew and the more she wanted to please me. A trainer wants to be able to rely on his dog's "face value"—what is known to be true about the dog's likes, wants, fears, and so forth. Shadow's face value was simply that she wanted to be wherever I was, and I built upon that foundation. Within a few short weeks—less than thirty days, actually—my relationship with Shadow grew to the point that I could begin teaching her to do more than follow me around the backyard. She eventually grew into a loving, obedient dog. I discovered at this young age the importance of building trust with a dog *before* trying to teach her to jump through hoops or drive a Nissan. To this day, I base my training principles on trust and the importance of knowing your dog. What I learned from Shadow has been paying off for decades.

Laying the Foundation

In the first couple of hours you've spent with your dog, you've already learned a little about his personality. Over the next thirty days, you will learn a whole lot more, and, most importantly, you will focus on building that ever-so-valuable relationship and trust. This is the most important lesson you can take from this book.

People see me working with my dog in seminars and expos, and

How do you train a dog to be reliable off leash? Build a relationship of trust so that he wants to be with you and please you.

they think that I must have some sort of special gift to be able to train my dog the way I do. In my mind, however, there is no gift involved. I get results for one simple reason: I am my dog's best friend. Because of that, he wants to make me happy. Successful training is all about the relationship.

In fact, training animals is no different than teaching people. The best teachers are the ones who get to know the students and develop meaningful relationships with them. Like great teachers, the best animal trainers I have been around were the ones who made the effort to learn about the animals they were training and to develop excellent relationships with them. By becoming the animals' friends, they created a foundation on which to build the trust that is so essential to successful training.

You now know the importance of a bond with regard to training animals in general, but why is it so important in training dogs in particular? Because a dog is totally different from any other animal in that he *wants* to please you and *wants* to be your friend. The *want* is a very important point here. Creating the bond and getting your dog to a place where he *wants* to make you happy is 99 percent of training. It lays an incredible foundation for everything you do with your dog!

Think about it. How much easier would training be if your dog had a dog who had a burning desire to please you before you ever began to train him? Compare that with a dog who has no desire to be around you or a dog who is not into the training session whatsoever. Any successful dog trainer will tell you that when you have an animal who wants to please you and make you happy, training is much easier and more fun.

One of the biggest mistakes an owner can make is training his dog before a relationship is established. If you have not spent enough time with your dog, you do not yet know him well enough to successfully train him. You don't know what your dog likes and dislikes, what he might be afraid of, or what he responds to best. When you begin to train a dog before you know him, you set yourself up for some major problems down the road.

Do not confuse the training of actual behaviors (*sit, stay, come, heel*) with problem-solving and preventative training. In the first thirty-day period, you are going to deal with house-training and other issues.

The time that you spend with your dog and everything you learn about him during the first thirty days form the basis for future training.

The Three Phases of Training

There are three phases involved in the dog's first thirty days at home with you: getting to know the animal, developing a relationship, and building trust. These three phases go hand in hand, and it is very important that you take the time to follow through with each one before continuing on to the next. You cannot build trust unless you've developed a relationship with the dog, and you cannot develop a relationship with the dog until you get to know him.

PHASE 1

GETTING TO KNOW THE DOG

This first phase will last from four to seven days. All you are doing during this time is getting to know the dog and learning as much as you possibly can about him. You want to identify your dog's likes, such as particular treats, certain kinds of toys, walks, meeting people, and meeting other dogs. To determine these, experiment with a variety of treats and toys. Introduce your dog to people outside the family and to other animals. Even make note of where he likes to sleep. This is how you will learn about your dog's favorite items and activities.

Your dog will not like everything. Remember, people have baggage, and so do dogs—some more than others. So while you're finding out what your dog likes, you'll also be finding out what he doesn't like. Your dog might not like certain people (such as people in uniform), other dogs, or moving objects such as motorcycles or skateboards.

During this phase, you'll also be observing your dog to determine his "color" based on the criteria discussed in Chapter 5.

Food is the way to the heart of many a dog. What treats get your dog's tail wagging?

PHASE 2

DEVELOPING A RELATIONSHIP

During this next phase, you will be taking ten to fourteen days to develop a great relationship with your dog. How will you accomplish this? You will do so by remembering the treats, the toys, the walks, the people, and other animals he likes and incorporating them into the dog's life during this phase.

At the same time, you will take into account the things that your dog does not like. If he does not like skateboards, cars, or people in uniform, you are going to eliminate those from your dog's daily life for the next couple of weeks.

You will also consider your dog's color. If your dog is Red or Orange, you know that there is a certain way you should act—firm and calm—around him to keep him under control. If you have a Green or Blue dog, he will need to be motivated and encouraged. A Yellow dog, as mentioned in the previous chapter, will likely just *go with the flow.*

Think about this phase from your dog's point of view. By doing nothing more than eliminating the things that the dog doesn't like

Building a relationship extends to all members of the family. When you find something that your dog likes to do, everyone should participate.

and incorporating the things that he does like, you are now setting the dog up to want to be around you. Do you think that if you continue to follow this plan for the next couple of weeks that the dog will be even happier to spend time with you? Absolutely, and that is what will take us into the last phase.

PHASE 3

BUILDING TRUST

As you enter this last phase, you have a dog who looks forward to being with you. You are now going to build on your relationship so that he not only wants to spend time with you but also begins to trust you. When you come home, the dog's tail may be wagging, he may be pacing in excitement, or he may be bouncing around in anticipation. These actions are all signs of an animal who is *in a great place,* and they come from the fact that over the last few weeks you've become a huge part of this dog's life. This is something you achieved by doing what you were supposed to do during the two previous phases.

Once you have your dog's trust, there's no limit to what the two of you can do together.

You are going to amplify this relationship even more by continuing to do everything you did in Phase 2 as well as by working with your dog to help him deal with any issues he may have. During this stage, it is essential that you continue to socialize your dog and expose him to as many different things as possible. If you there is something that your dog does not like or is afraid of, this is the time to deal with it. For example, helping a dog overcome a fear of an object or person will increase his trust in you. We will discuss all of this in more detail in Chapter 7.

7 desensitization, exposure, and socialization

Lights! Camera! Chaos! Bright hot lights, noisy moving cameras, familiar and strange humans, applause from more strange humans. That pretty much describes a day working on a television set from a canine point of view, and it can be overwhelming for a dog who isn't prepared for it. Before a dog is trained to be a TV actor, he should be well socialized and exposed to many different people, places, things, and noises so that he is desensitized to them.

That's what I did with Bear, a dog I trained from 1988 to 1992 for the top-ten NBC sitcom *Empty Nest*, in which he portrayed the family dog, "Dreyfuss." When I started training Bear, he was a very Orange dog, but halfway through the second season, he became a reliable Yellow dog, which is ideal for an animal actor.

Dogs like routine and a predictable environment. The schedule for this Saturday night show ran from Wednesday, when the new script was distributed, through Tuesday, when the episode was filmed in front of a live audience.

Exposure can be as easy as taking walks in different places and including your dogs in things you do every day.

To say that Bear became acclimated to the set, the cast, and the studio would be an understatement. One day, we were filming a particularly long scene in which Bear was scripted to get up and exit the scene about two minutes into it. A simple task for Bear—or so I thought!

I put Bear in his usual spot before the scene started and had him lie down. The actors started the scene, and he lay there as he was supposed to do and as we had rehearsed all week long. About thirty seconds before I was to give him his cue to exit the set, I noticed that his eyes were half open. The actors' energy and all of the excitement of the live audience didn't seem to have their usual effect on Bear. Was he actually falling asleep? There wasn't a thing I could do to rouse him, and as the dialogue continued, his eyes continued to close.

The moment of truth came, and I gave Bear his cue. I might as well have been cuing the wall or the chair! Bear slept right through it. The cast waited for him to exit—and nothing. Bear had clearly become *too* comfortable in his work environment. The director yelled "Cut!" as the cast, crew, and audience burst into laughter while Bear happily snoozed away.

I recalled this incident years later when I was thinking about a title for a book I was writing on the training of rescued dogs such as Bear: *Take 2*, of course!

The Essentials of Exposure, Desensitization, and Socialization

It is essential that, as a new pet owner, you expose your dog to as many things as possible, provided that the dog has had all of his vaccinations. This chapter will help you with:

- **Understanding exposure and socialization**
- **Understanding desensitization**
- **Desensitizing your dog to people**
- **Desensitizing your dog to moving objects**
- **Desensitizing your dog to stationary objects**
- **Socializing your dog with cats**
- **Socializing your dog with other dogs**

Before I start explaining how to implement these concepts, I want to give you my definition of these very important aspects of dog training.

Exposure and socialization—Exposure and socialization go hand in hand. When we are exposing and socializing a dog, we are simply putting him in an environment that is different from his own familiar environment and having him see, hear, and interact with different beings (human and animal), objects, and places. One of the most natural and important examples of this is simply taking your dog for a walk on a different street or around a different block.

Through training with the author, Bear (pictured) became a mellow Yellow and a successful TV sitcom star.

Desensitization—Desensitizing a dog is the action of giving the dog a stress-free experience with certain objects and people. Desensitization addresses issues that stem from a lack of exposure and socialization. A good example is a dog who lives indoors and whose only time outdoors is for brief potty trips in the backyard. If the animal rarely gets a chance to go anywhere other than his home, everyday distractions can become foreign to him very quickly. Things that *we* see as normal, such as a car going by, a bicyclist, a postman in uniform, or a person wearing a baseball cap, can cause the dog to feel uneasy when he does get the chance to go somewhere new and see these things, because they are not part of his usual life and routine.

There's so much you can do with a dog who's well adjusted and with whom you have a strong bond.

How uncomfortable and frightened the dog becomes depends on the color of the dog. A Green dog who is never exposed to anything and has not been socialized will most likely exhibit some fear when taken out of his normal living area and introduced to things that are foreign to him. A Blue dog's fear response will be amplified.

A Yellow dog can actually move away from the center of the color spectrum toward Green if he doesn't get proper exposure and socialization. Make no mistake about it—a Yellow Dog can absolutely develop fears and uncertainties if he never sees new places and objects.

An Orange dog with slight aggressive tendencies can become more aggressive if he sees something unfamiliar that makes him uneasy. A Red dog, being further away from the center of the color spectrum, can develop an

Dogs are naturally curious about the many sights, sounds, and smells of the great outdoors.

even more severe response. A great example of this is a Red dog who is always kept in the backyard without any opportunities to interact and socialize. Some neighborhood kids tease the dog through the fence every day for a few years, and the dog constantly barks at them. Let me ask you a question: if sometime down the road, this dog escapes from his yard, whom is he likely to go after first? No exposure and no positive interactions with strangers, combined with the kids' teasing him and making him uneasy, can cause severe fear and aggression problems in a dog who is left in the backyard in the same situation every day.

One of the reasons for this chapter is to fill you in on something that you might not know about dogs—they have incredible, almost computerlike, memories. For example, your dog will remember that sometimes when you go to the refrigerator and open it, you toss him a piece of cheese. You only have to do this a few times before the dog will begin to follow you to the refrigerator every time and patiently wait for his piece of cheese.

The same thing applies to the things in your dog's life that might make him uncomfortable and uneasy. Sometimes all it takes is one bad experience. For example, you take your dog for a walk, and suddenly a kid on a skateboard appears from behind, startling you. If you are startled, you can be certain that your dog will be, too. If this situation happens again, it can magnify the dog's fear. The further the dog is from the center of the color spectrum, the more likely it is that his fear will increase in similar situations.

In my first book, *What Color is Your Dog?*, and in the previous chapter, I discussed that one of the mistakes made by many new dog owners is trying to train their dogs before establishing a relationship. I talked about the important three phases you'll go through in your dog's first thirty days at home with you: getting to know your dog, developing a relationship, and building trust. During this first thirty days, you'll be taking notice of your dog's likes and dislikes, and you must really be aware of the things that make your dog feel apprehensive. Many owners are simply not observant or aware when it comes to their dogs' insecurities. A mistake that owners might make is noticing a distraction and trying to deal with it during the four- to seven-day "getting-to-know-you" phase, which should be reserved strictly for learning about each other.

In the second phase, as you're building your relationship, you create a positive environment by incorporating what your dog likes and eliminating what he doesn't like. During this time, you can certainly continue to expose him to new things and socialize him, but don't *deal with desensitization to things he dislikes*. Remember, this is the relationship-building phase, which should be as positive as you can make it, so you are not going to put the dog in situations that you know are going to make him uncomfortable. Desensitization can begin after the third phase, once we have earned the dog's trust.

During the first three to four weeks, it is essential that all dogs, regardless of color, get some sort of exposure and socialization to outside stimuli. Some dogs need more exposure than others do. A simple way to think of it is to picture the color spectrum. In the center, we have mellow Yellow. Although this dog needs socialization and exposure, just like any dog does, he will likely need the least desensitization training. Yellow dogs are naturally laid back and not as likely to be bothered by distractions.

As we start moving outward on the spectrum in either direction, we find the Green and Orange dogs. Green dogs are going to be a little more apprehensive toward both stationary objects and moving objects, such as skateboards, cars, and bicycles. Green dogs might also have some apprehension toward people. Blue dogs are going to have the same types of apprehension that the Green dogs do; the only difference is that the Blue dog's fear is more intense, as he is further away from the mellow Yellow center of the spectrum. Dealing with some of these issues will certainly be more challenging with a Blue dog than with a Green dog.

Moving objects may cause a dog to be fearful or may incite his prey drive and desire to chase.

Orange dogs are a little more high-strung, so they may become aggressive toward the object or person making them uncomfortable. Unless an Orange dog is desensitized to the source of his fear early on, his aggressive reactions can escalate over time with repeated exposures. The Red dog, being further from the center of the spectrum, will be more challenging than an Orange dog. If an Orange dog can be fearful or somewhat aggressive, then the Red dog can have the same types of responses, but magnified. Remember that the further your dog is from the center of the spectrum in either direction, the more time for exposure and socialization he will need.

Desensitization—The Training

When you are desensitizing a dog to something, you are teaching him to not be afraid of or uncomfortable around a certain person or object. To do this effectively, you need to understand your dog and how he expresses his fear. His reactions and behaviors depend upon his personality and makeup.

There are three things that most dogs will do out of fear: run, hide, and bark. If the fear is allowed to escalate, or if the dog feels that he cannot get away from the source of his fear, a cooler-colored dog will go further away from the center of the spectrum, possibly striking out of fear and consequently biting. The same can be said for the warmer-colored (Red and Orange) dogs. Although they are, to some degree, high-strung and thus perceived as more confident, they still may show fear of some things. As with the cooler-colored dogs, if the fear escalates, a Red or Orange dog can respond aggressively toward the source of his fear.

FEAR OF PEOPLE

If your dog is afraid of people, one of the first things you need to ask yourself is, "How long has this been going on?" The longer the dog has been exhibiting his fear, the more difficult that fear will be to correct. With a recently adopted shelter or rescue dog, youw have limited to no information about the dog's history. You have to assume, though, that if the animal expresses some sort of fear around people, the fear has come from a negative experience in his past. The dog's fear may stem from the way he was initially trained, the lack of relationship between the dog and his previous owner, or perhaps the way he was cared for in his former home.

Aggression Advice

The best thing to do with a dog who has the potential for aggression is to work with a trainer specializing in aggressive behavior. Do not waste your money or your time on a dog trainer who does not have an in-depth understanding of aggression.

Try to identify what it is about certain people that frightens him. Is your dog afraid only of men, of women, of people who wear glasses, or of people carrying umbrellas? Another factor to note is the location of the animal when he exhibits a fearful reaction. Does it happen only in your home? Does it happen only at the park? Does it happen everywhere? Does it happen everywhere except in your home? These are important facts to know before you try to deal with the fear behavior.

No matter what color dog you have, you must not allow his fear to escalate. A Green dog can easily become a Blue dog, an Orange dog can easily become a Red dog, and Blue and Red dogs can easily become even more extreme in their behavior if allowed to manifest their fear over and over again. Remember, we want dogs to move toward mellow Yellow in the center of the spectrum. The further the dog is from Yellow when you begin training, the bigger the challenges you will face in dealing with the issue at hand.

No matter what color dog I am training, I am always inclined to begin with redirection. Redirection is simply shifting the dog's focus to something else—something enjoyable and something the dog will find more interesting than the source of his fear.

Before you begin, find a high-value treat, something your dog just absolutely *goes crazy* over. It may be a piece of steak, chicken, or cheese. The treat should be something that the dog gets only when you are dealing with this problem, and given to him only by an individual with whom he has an issue (that is, a person he fears), not by you.

STEP 1

First, you need to enlist the help of a friend for this training; it should be someone whom the dog does not know and who represents the type of person that makes the dog uneasy—a man, a person wearing a hat, a person

Hats, glasses, and bows...this dog doesn't mind indulging in a little dress-up fun.

wearing a raincoat. This person should agree to be available to help you with several training sessions each day during your dog's desensitization training.

Keep some bite-sized pieces of your high-value treat in a small plastic bag. Take the dog for a walk, and when you encounter your helper, give him or her a treat to offer to the dog. Let the dog approach the person rather than having the person approach the dog; let the dog take the treat on his own terms. The person must *not* get excited or try to encourage the dog; in fact, the person should not talk to, try to pet, or make eye contact with the dog. In this scenario, the other person is functioning basically as a prop; you almost want the person to seem like an inanimate object.

Reward with Care

When using redirection, it is essential that you never unintentionally reward the dog for exhibiting any aggression or barking. Pay attention to the timing of your reward, and always be aware of the behavior that you are rewarding.

You want the dog to take the treat from this person with as little fear as possible. As soon as the person gives the dog the treat, he or she should walk away. This should be a very short training session. Once the dog takes the treat, the training session is over, and you and the dog can return home. Try to put in three to six sessions like this each day for the first few days.

If you think about this from your dog's perspective, he gets a treat from a person, and then the person leaves. That's it! And since this really cool treat does not come from you, and only comes from this particular individual, what do you think is going to happen the next time your dog sees this person? The dog will most likely wonder if the person has that really cool treat that he dog likes so much.

This is the beginning of your dog's desensitization training. How much time it takes to make the dog comfortable around people who frighten him will depend on the severity of your pet's fear. Over time, the dog will begin to look forward to seeing this person, because that person always has something positive for the dog. It is essential for you to understand that everything we are doing at this point is on the dog's terms.

When the dog is a little more comfortable with the person, let the person start to give the dog a few treats at a time, maybe spending ten seconds with the dog. Eventually, the person can offer his or her hand to the dog, and if the dog indicates that he wants to be petted, the person can give the dog a simple stroke. Whether the person is just offering treats or is petting the dog, it's important for the person to always walk away after ten seconds, *leaving the dog wanting more.*

By kneeling and avoiding eye contact, the helper assumes a position that encourages the dog to approach her without fear.

STEP 2

Once your dog is consistently comfortable with this person coming to him, giving him a treat, and walking away, the next step is to have the person start spending more time with the dog. Something that works well is to have the person take a few treats and just kneel down and let the dog come to him or her. While kneeling, your helper gives the dog a treat, waits a few seconds, gives the dog another treat, waits a few—maybe ten—seconds more, gives one more treat, and then gets up and walks away. During this phase, it is imperative that the person is still limiting eye contact with the dog.

STEPS 3 AND 4

In the third phase of this training, you'll keep doing the same thing but gradually increasing the amount of eye contact that your helper has with the dog. Keep the sessions short and positive. Once you have made progress with the eye contact, it's on to the fourth phase, in which you'll start building the length of time of the training sessions to about two minutes. Two minutes is a long time for a dog to keep eating treats, so I recommend that you decrease the treats to one treat every fifteen or twenty seconds. It also helps to train when the dog is hungry. You may feel guilty delaying your dog's meal for the training session, but a full dog will be less likely to eat the treats, thus defeating the purpose of this type of training.

Remember, as before, the person must allow the dog to approach him or her. A good idea is to have the person sit on the ground.

STEP 5

This is the last step. By now, the dog is becoming more and more comfortable with your helper. Start having the person accompany you and your dog when you go for walks. Every once in a while along the walk, have the person give the dog a treat. If the dog will accept petting, the person can pet the dog.

Remember that all dogs are different, as is the reaction that an individual dog will have to an individual person. The dog may get used to this person a little more quickly than he will get used to others. Most importantly, do not rush the process. Take your time and work at your dog's speed.

FEAR OF OBJECTS

If you find that your dog has a fear of certain objects, you need to start by asking the same question you'd ask if he were afraid of a person: "How long has this been going on?" The longer the dog has been fearful of something, the more you will have to work with him to help him get over it. You may not know the cause of an adopted dog's fear. Some dogs are nervous by nature, and their fear doesn't necessarily stem from a bad experience. It is also important to realize that what is stressful to humans is not necessarily traumatic to dogs; nonetheless, bad experiences can have a lasting impact on dogs.

To get your dog over his fear, you'll first need to identify what he is afraid of. See if you can single out a specific category of objects, such moving objects like cars, skateboards, and motorcycles. It doesn't have to be objects that move; your dog may be afraid of something stationary. You also want to determine where the dog exhibits this fear. Is he afraid of an object at home? Is it something found only in a specific place, such as the park or a certain corner of the yard? Does your dog have the fear reaction everywhere you go? You'll need this information before trying to deal with the behavior.

Remember, as we discussed in the previous section about fear of people, the longer a dog's fear is allowed to escalate, the more a dog will start to move toward the outer edges of the color spectrum. A Green dog can turn Blue and start to exhibit fear aggression. A Blue dog can start having more intense fear reactions. The same happens on the other side of the spectrum: an Orange dog turns Red, and a Red dog becomes extremely Red. The only difference is that this is called *prey aggression* rather than *fear aggression*.

You might notice that I don't mention Yellow dogs here. The reason is that the mellow Yellows are not easily spooked, so owners of Yellow dogs are not likely to have problems with their dogs being afraid of objects (or other things, such as noises).

Just as in training a dog to eliminate the fear of people, you'll begin with redirection—turning the dog's focus to something other than what is causing him to be fearful. In doing so, you want to teach the dog that this is something positive, not something to be afraid of.

As discussed in the previous section, you need to identify a high-value treat that the dog goes crazy over. Remember, this will be a special treat given to your dog only when you are training him to become desensitized to a specific object or other thing. The treat will be offered to your dog only by an individual with whom we will teach him to associate the problem object, never by you. This way, we are redirecting the dog's focus away from the source of his fear to a person who has something the dog wants. The training technique for a dog who is afraid of moving objects, such as cars, motorcycles, bicycles, and skateboards, is different from the training technique used for a dog who is afraid of stationary objects. Hats and umbrellas are two stationary objects that commonly cause a dog to be fearful.

MOVING OBJECTS—STEP 1

To get started, have your treats and your helper ready; the dog will be with you on leash. Remember, our goal is to get the dog to associate something positive (the person with the treat) with something he currently views as negative (the moving object). We want the dog to eventually take the treat from the person without being concerned about the moving object.

In the first step, keep the moving object in a stationary position at a distance at which the dog does not show any fear of the object. It is best not to take your dog to the object at this point in training. Instead, have your helper walk to the object, stand next to it for a few seconds, and then walk to the dog and give the dog a treat. Repeat this three or four times, or until the dog is consistently taking the treat without showing any fear.

The helper first moves the object only slightly until the dog is comfortable with the movement.

MOVING OBJECTS—STEP 2

Now we will have our helper start up, but not move, the vehicle, if the moving object is a motorized vehicle. The person will leave the motor on for five to ten seconds and then shut it off. With a nonmotorized object, such as a skateboard or motorcycle, the person will still just stand next to the object, as in the previous step. After the allotted time of allowing the motor to run or standing next to the object, the person will walk away from object and give the dog a treat. Only move

When the dog is comfortable with the object in motion, you can eventually bring him closer to the object, decreasing the distance gradually.

on to the next step when the dog is focused on the person coming to give him a treat, not on the object. Try to put in three sessions, no more, like this each day for the first few days.

MOVING OBJECTS—STEP 3

In this step, we are going to start moving the object slightly, parallel to the dog. Have the person start the car or motorcycle, move it about a foot, turn it off, walk over to the dog, and give him a treat. It works the same way with bicycles or skateboards (except for the startup part, of course!).

MOVING OBJECTS—STEP 4

Now we are going to start moving the object a little more with each training session. Start by moving the object 2 feet, then 4 feet, and so on. Only increase the distance if the dog was OK with the previous distance. Soon you'll be able to move the object around as you normally would, and the dog should be comfortable with it.

After you move the object a given distance, keep it stationary with the person standing next to it. The dog will now have to walk to the person to receive his treat.

Remember that every dog's fear of moving objects is different, so tailor your training to your dog's degree of fear. Keep the sessions short so that you always end with the dog's "wanting more."

STATIONARY OBJECTS—STEP 1

One of the best parts of teaching your dog to get over his fear of stationary objects is that you can do it on your own—no helper required, just a leash. As in the other desensitization exercises, you'll have your bag of high-value treats that you'll give to the dog only during these training sessions. Again, the goal is for the dog to associate something positive (the treat) with the object that he views as negative.

Put the object on the ground at a distance from the dog that he is OK with. If your dog is not fearful at a distance of 10 feet away from the object, place the object 10 feet away from where you and the dog will stand. Put a few treats on the ground around you, and allow the dog to eat the treats, encouraging him if needed. When the dog is consistent in eating the treats with no fear or hesitation, end the training session.

STATIONARY OBJECTS—STEP 2

Place the treats on the ground a few feet away from you, somewhere between you and the feared object. If the dog takes the treats with no concern about the object, next time place the treats a few feet closer to the object. When your dog is consistent, repeat this last step and end the training session. Put in no more than three sessions this first day, always starting off with the treats close to you on the ground.

TOP: At first, the dog eats treats from the ground right in front of him, still at a good distance from the object. BOTTOM: With each successive step in training, the treats—and thus, the dog—get closer to the object.

STATIONARY OBJECTS—STEP 3

Now we are simply going to start moving the treats a little closer to the object each time. You might have ended the last session with the dog 4 feet away from you. Your goal should then be to end the next session with the dog 6 feet away from you (and thus 2 feet closer to the object). If you started with the dog at a distance of 10 feet from the object, he is now closer to the object than he is to you. By keeping the training sessions short, you always leave the dog "wanting more."

TOP: Scatter the treats around the object. BOTTOM: The dog should be so engrossed in eating the treats that he shows no fear of the object right next to him.

STATIONARY OBJECTS—STEP 4

Our goal now is to shorten the distance between you and the object by half, so if you started off with the dog 10 feet away from the object in Step 1, start this session with the dog 5 feet away. Place the treats on the ground a few feet away from you. Because the object is only 5 feet away, the dog is now taking the treats at a distance of only about 2 feet from the object. When he's OK with this, put the treats just 1 foot away from the object. Repeat this and end the session.

STATIONARY OBJECTS—STEP 5

In this next session, we are going to start with the object even closer, about 3 feet away. Put the treats on the ground, 1 foot away from you. If the dog is OK with that, put the treats on the ground next to the object. If your dog is OK with that, start placing the treats around the object. Once your dog is fine with taking treats from around the object, the training sessions will become almost like games to him. Repeat this a few more times and end the session.

STATIONARY OBJECTS—STEP 6

In this step, simply start slowly lifting the object off the ground. You will no longer be putting treats on the ground. The first time you lift the object, crouch down and raise it just slightly. Reward the dog with a treat as you put the object back on the ground. Each time you do this, lift the object a little higher, and always reward the dog with a treat as you put it down. Keep repeating this step until you are standing up with the object.

LEFT: Start by lifting the object just a few inches off the ground. RIGHT: Increase the height as your dog becomes comfortable, making sure to reward him with a treat each time you put the object down.

STATIONARY OBJECTS—STEP 7

In this last phase, we are going to lift the object, carry it parallel to the dog a few feet in front of him, and then place it on the ground. Start by picking up the object, carrying it a few feet, and putting it down. Reward the dog with a treat when you put the object down. Each time you repeat this, carry the object a little farther away and end by placing the object down and rewarding the dog. If the dog is consistently comfortable with this, carry the object and reward the dog while you are still holding it. Once you can do this, the behavior is trained.

This technique is an extensive step-by-step approach to eliminating your dog's fear of an object. How quickly or how slowly you progress through each step will depend on the degree of your dog's fear. Never rush your dog; work at his pace and take your time.

Socialization

Sometimes it is a good idea to see things through your dog's eyes. If you are a little uncomfortable meeting new people in a new environment, you know how unpleasant that can be. Everyone has likely been in an awkward social situation at one time or another. Now imagine that you're a dog, you're feeling a little unsure, and all of a sudden you have a cat hissing at you or another dog jumping all over you. It can end up being a horrible experience. This section will help you make the best of that very valuable first meeting between your new dog and your cat or resident dog.

SOCIALIZING A CAT AND A DOG

If you have a cat, and you have just brought your dog home, you will need to "formally" introduce the two pets. *Do not just put them together and assume that everything will be OK*! If you put them together right off the bat, without a supervised introduction, there is only a very slight chance that it won't end in disaster. If your dog has a high prey drive, he might actually go after the cat, which could end up in one or both animals' being hurt, and it could also have a very negative emotional impact on your cat. Or your high-octane cat, who's feeling territorial, might go after your new Blue dog.

This first meeting lays the foundation for the animals' long-term relationship, so you must handle it carefully. The future peace of your household is at stake! So let's discuss a great way to introduce your dog and cat.

Stationary Introductions

Let me start by reminding you of what I said in the beginning of the book about *prey drive*. We know that certain dogs have a higher prey drive than others and that prey drive is driven by sights, sounds, and odors. The combination of a high-prey-drive dog with a cat who wants to run means that the dog is going to want to chase the cat. Sometimes the chain of events starts with the cat's jumping off a table or a windowsill. The high-prey-drive dog's instinct will kick

With some attention to socialization, all members of the family—human and animal—can live harmoniously in a multiple-pet household.

in, and his first reaction will be to want to chase what he perceives as "prey." That's why you want to you have some way of controlling one of the animals as you begin your introductions. One way to do this is to have the dog on leash when you introduce him to the cat. If the hair on your cat's back is standing up, if the cat arches her back, if she appears as if she wants to run, or if she stares at or starts stalking the dog, you will know that she is uncomfortable or afraid.

For the first introduction, keep the dog 10–15 feet from the cat. How your cat reacts at this distance will give you a good indication of her general attitude toward the dog and how quickly you may be able to move the introductions along.

If the dog is lunging and wanting toward to the cat, bring him back to a distance where he is no longer trying to get to the cat. The dog's reaction will also help you decide how quickly or slowly you want to progress in bringing the two of them together.

If both the dog and the cat are OK at your initial distance of 10–15 feet away, I would just stay there for the next fifteen or twenty minutes. Then take the dog away from the area, thus ending the first training session.

Assuming that the dog and cat were both OK during the first training session, the next training session should begin the same way: with the dog on leash at a distance of 10–15 feet from the cat. If they are OK at that distance for ten minutes, walk the dog a little closer, between 7–10 feet away. End the training session once they are relaxed at this distance.

During the next session, we want to get the dog to the point where he is only 5 feet away from the cat. Take note of the cat's attitude toward the dog at this distance. Sometimes at this point the cat will begin to calm down and not focus as much on the dog. If that happens, celebrate!

Walking Introductions

If the cat is OK with the dog 5 feet away, it is time to start walking your dog on leash around the house. You can let the leash drag on the ground, but make sure that you can pick it up and grab it if the dog starts going near the cat. Never let the dog just wander without the leash, and always be aware of where both animals are.

As the dog and cat get more and more comfortable, you can start increasing the length of the training session, still letting the leash drag. After a few more days, you can take the leash off the dog if you feel that the time is right to do so. It is up to you to read the body language of your dog and your cat. As they get more comfortable around one another, you will definitely notice a change in the interaction between them.

So much of this really depends on the dog. If the dog does not do anything to make the cat nervous, then the cat will remain calm and, thus, the dog should also remain calm. If, on the other hand, the dog is doing something to make the cat nervous and uncomfortable, the cat's nervousness will in turn be picked up by the dog.

I think one of the mistakes that people make is progressing too quickly through the steps. Sometimes owners do a few sessions in which the animals are 10 feet away from each other and everything is OK, so they think that they can stop doing the gradual socialization sessions. You really need to take your time with this to let the animals truly become comfortable with each other.

SOCIALIZING TWO DOGS

Earlier in the book, I mentioned that if you have a dog and are thinking of bringing a new one into the house, you must make sure that your resident dog gets along with other dogs. Even if your dog does generally like other dogs, you still can't just bring your new dog home and let the two of them loose together. You don't know how they will react. But odds that are your resident dog will be territorial. He thinks of your home as *his* territory, and all of a sudden, another dog just shows up. If the resident dog reacts in a territorial and/or aggressive manner, you could have a fight on your hands, putting both dogs at risk of injury. Not only that, but if this is the first thing that happens between these dogs, it will not bode well for their future relationship. I want to give you every opportunity to make your new dog's homecoming a positive experience for both your new and your resident dog. The following steps are intended to be done using a screen door that opens up into a fenced yard. If you don't have a fenced yard or if you live in an apartment with no screen door, you'll do the introduction training with both dogs on leash. You'll be with the new dog, and you'll need a helper for the resident dog.

Walking two dogs at the same time is a good way to start getting them accustomed to each other.

The First Introduction

I like to start the introductions through a screen door, and I recommend keeping both dogs on their leashes even though the screen door will be shut.

> ### Let's Take a Walk
>
> **A great way to socialize two dogs is to take them for walks together. This allows the dogs to get used to being around each other without making a *formal* introduction. It is essential when you walk the dogs together that you do not make it about the introduction. The only thing you are going to be doing is having them both walk with you at the same time. I suggest keeping a good distance of 5 or 6 feet between the dogs.**

One of the reasons I recommend introducing them through the screen door is that the dogs will naturally start to sniff each other. Dogs learn a lot about other dogs simply by doing so. And you want them to get as much information about each other as possible. Because of their incredible sense of smell, they will learn a lot more about each other than we can imagine.

You also will learn a lot during these first few minutes by observing the dogs' body language and actions. There are two specific places on your dog's coat that can change in appearance out of excitement or aggression: one is the area around the shoulder blades/back of neck, and the other is the area around the base of the tail. When the hairs in one or both of these areas stand on end, it's known as *hackling*. This is a dog's way of appearing larger to another dog, sometimes out of aggression and other times as a natural way to protect himself.

After a few minutes, you may see both dogs get a little playful and almost puppyish with each other. This normally is a very good sign, but it might not be a good sign if what you perceive as being play is actually aggression. It is so important to watch the dogs' body language. Are they showing teeth or snarling? Is there any growling? Is one dog's hair hackled around the shoulder blades and the base of the tail? These are some things of which you need to be aware.

The Second Introduction

The second time you introduce the dogs to each other, you'll still keep the screen door between them. If they continue to be comfortable around each other, I recommend taking off the leashes. This will give them a chance to move around a little more naturally and still smell each other, but they won't yet have the opportunity to be in the same area with each other. Do this type of introduction three or four times, with each session lasting for about ten to fifteen minutes.

The Actual Introduction

Before you make the actual introduction, in which the dogs meet face to face with nothing between them, I want to share with you something that I have done for many years. If you have a backyard, I would recommend buying a few supplies before this introduction. You can buy a nozzle and an on-and-off switch that attaches to a garden hose; such items are available at home-improvement and hardware stores. Attach these to your hose and turn the hose on, keeping the switch in the "off" position. If you turn the switch to "on," a stream of water will come out.

This gives you some form of control when you put the dogs together, and if either dog gets a little aggressive or overly playful with the other, you can spray the dog gently with the hose. Hopefully you never have to use the hose, but it can really come in handy.

Notice how the dogs start to interact with each other; you hope to see that playful puppy attitude. You might see one dog run up to the other and kind of jostle him back and forth; this is an invitation to play, and sometimes it takes effort on the part of one dog to initiate play. One more tip: eliminate the risk of any possessive aggression on the resident dog's part by removing all toys from the backyard until the animals have been together for a while and are really comfortable playing with one another.

This is the introduction process that I have used for many years. Remember, though, that there are *no absolutes* when it comes to dog behavior. Every situation is different, but that is what makes the socialization process fun and unique. Just remember to take your time when socializing.

8 before you train

It's ironic that I am writing about problem-solving and house-training when I had such a challenging time with my dog Foster, the little gray terrier mix that you see in many pictures with me and in my books. I talked a little about his rescue story earlier in the book. Although no one told me his history, I could easily deduce it from his actions: he had been allowed to relieve himself on everything and everybody and allowed to chew on everything and everybody. His previous owners had likely tormented him with a broom, so I had to be very careful every time I wanted to sweep. Foster also was a little aggressive. There was no question that Foster had some big problems.

From the beginning, the one thing I made sure to do with Foster was keep him out of situations in which he could engage in, and thus escalate, his bad behaviors. Over the course of time, his behavior began to change. The chewing stopped, the barking stopped, the fear of the broom lessened, and—best of all—the urinating on my leg stopped. In the years since then, Foster has become the star of my training demonstrations, traveling with me to perform in my seminars across the country. It just goes to show you that underneath behavior issues can be dogs with great potential.

When it comes to dealing with problem behaviors, my philosophy has always been to understand not only how to stop these behaviors but also why and how these behaviors occur in the first place. Whatever behavior problem you are dealing with, now or in the future, remember what was said earlier: most adopted dogs come with emotional/behavioral baggage, some of them more so than others. You're also going to find that certain dogs take a little longer to figure things out than others do.

When I talk to people, I find quite often that they think that the specific problems they are encountering with their dogs is unique—that no one else has faced the same thing. I can almost guarantee you that the problem you are having with your dog is not yours alone.

Your dog may love the sound of his own voice, but will you and your neighbors be just as appreciative?

Right now, hundreds, if not thousands, of other dog owners are dealing with the very same problem that you are.

I think a lot of people have misconceptions about dog training. They seem to focus on what to do when the animal does something right and what to do when he does something wrong. We all know that when the animal does something right, we should reward him, but what about when he behaves inappropriately or develops bad behaviors? How should we react? People need to know the answer to this from day one because more often than not, when owners first get their dog, they find the dog doing more things wrong than right. If a new pet owner responds to an animal's undesirable behavior correctly, it not only teaches the dog right and wrong but also has a huge positive impact on the owner's relationship with his or her pet down the road.

Obedience Classes

Before I address how to deal with specific problems (see Chapter 9), you should understand that putting your dog through formal obedience training resolves many behavioral issues. You are giving your dog something positive to do with his energy, making him less inclined to act out inappropriately. Obedience training "takes the edge off" because you are challenging the dog's mind and body, which stimulates him, calms him, and builds his confidence.

Training Methods

When working on problem-solving with your dog, you will use one of three different styles of training—or a combination of them—in dealing with your specific behavior problem: preventative training, corrections, and redirection.

PREVENTATIVE TRAINING

As I have emphasized throughout this book, a dog will not develop bad behaviors if he is not given the opportunity to develop them. This means keeping him out of situations and places in which bad behavior can start. This is the basis of preventative training, which has proved very effective for thousands of dog owners. Preventative-training techniques—which are also about owners' learning to take certain steps—can also be used in behavior modification to deal with an existing problem.

To use the house-training example, if a dog has a problem urinating on the carpet and is allowed to wander unattended in the house, he will continue to urinate on the carpet. However, if your dog is safely confined, such as in a crate, when you're away, he does not have the opportunity to relieve himself on the carpet.

Similarly, if your dog gets into the trash can in the backyard, and he spends time alone in the backyard, he will keep getting into the trash. If, however, you store the trash can somewhere inaccessible to the dog, he won't have the opportunity to get into it.

Don't trust your dog to keep his nose and paws out of an accessible trash can. Prevent bad behavior by putting the trash where he can't get to it.

CORRECTIONS

A lot of people misunderstand what it is to give a "correction," so let me give you my people-friendly example. Let's say that you're teaching me a phrase in a foreign language. I say the phrase, and you interrupt me to tell me that I pronounced a word wrong. I start the phrase over, and this time I say the word correctly. What just happened is that you simply corrected my pronunciation, and I repeated the word and said it the right way. That's all a correction is. It is an interruption. *Do not let anyone tell you anything different.* If you think of a correction as punishment, and that stops you from correcting your dog for behavior problems, you will be confusing your dog. He will never understand what you want because he's not being taught right from wrong.

How you deliver a correction can vary greatly; delivery depends on the color and the specific problem of the dog you are training. With Blue, Green, and Yellow dogs, the correction will be milder. With a Red or Orange dog, you usually need to use a firmer correction.

For a dog, doing something incorrectly is a very important part of the learning process. It's another chance to learn right from wrong. The dog will never learn what you want if you don't praise him when he does well, nor will he learn what not to do if you do not correct his problem behavior. The bottom line is that it's OK for him to be wrong, as long as you let him know that he's wrong and show him the right thing to do.

REDIRECTION

When we talk about redirection, we simply mean that we're trying to stop a dog's inappropriate behavior by redirecting him into the right behavior. Redirection does not work with every dog, nor does it work with every behavior problem, but it can be extremely successful under the right circumstances. In redirection, you focus the dog's attention on something other than the undesirable behavior with something like a high-value treat. The catch? The only way for this to be successful is if the treat has more meaning to the dog than the desire to continue the bad behavior.

Let's assume that your dog is afraid of most people, and he barks at them when he sees them. Let's also assume that your dog loves chicken and steak. If your dog will accept a piece of chicken or steak

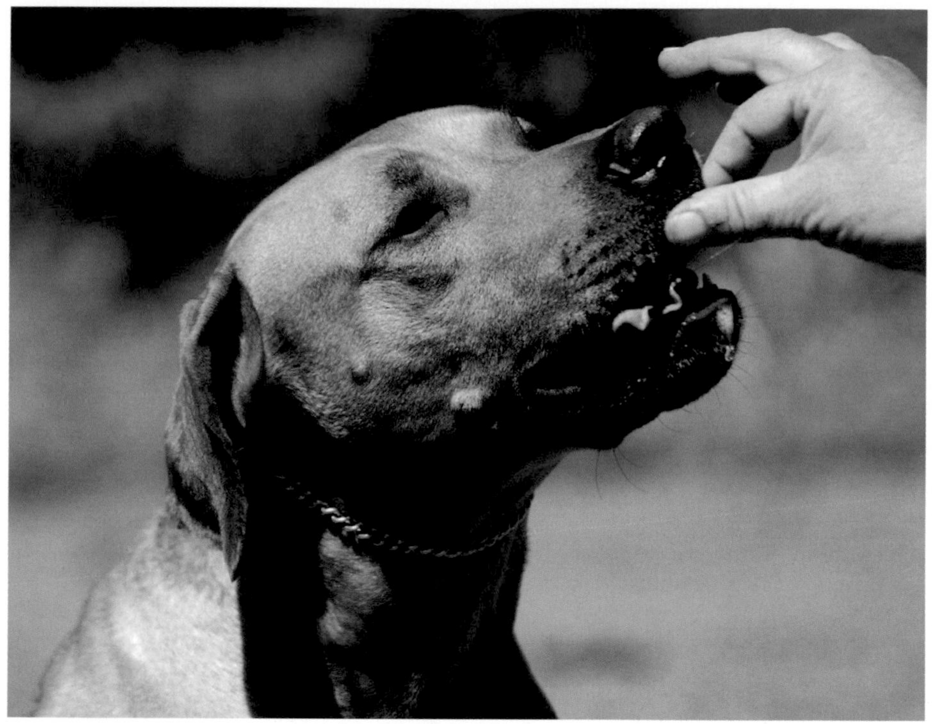

Many dogs respond well to redirection training, in which you use something that the dog likes to distract him into acceptable behavior.

from a person he likes, it can work to your advantage because you can to transfer that action of the dog's taking the treat to a person at whom the animal normally barks. That redirection of teaching the dog to focus on the treat that he will be getting rather than on barking can really work well with some dogs.

Be Aware!

It is imperative that you are aware of bad behavior as soon as it starts, which means that you need to be very observant. If you see your dog becoming possessive, barking, jumping on people, digging in the trash, or leaving "surprises" on your carpet, you need to deal with those behaviors right away. Remember that bad behaviors such as these can, if left unattended, escalate and become conditioned, or *learned*, behaviors. Once a bad behavior has been occurring so long that it becomes conditioned, it is very hard to retrain the correct behavior. It is important that everyone in the home is on board with rehabilitating the dog.

If your dog's fondness for his toys crosses the line and becomes possessive behavior, you must deal with it right away to prevent aggression from developing.

Among dogs, there are certain behavior problems that are more common than others. What varies from dog to dog is the severity of each specific problem. For example, one owner may have a dog who urinates in the house once a week, while another owner may have a dog who urinates in the house three times a day. It is the same behavior problem, but on totally different levels. Clearly, the person dealing with a dog who urinates inside three times a day has a much bigger problem on his hands than does the person with the dog who has a once-a-week accident. Yet if the second owner doesn't deal with the problem right away, that relatively minor problem will quickly become a major one.

With any behavior problem, you need to know how long it's been occurring. If the dog has been exhibiting the problem behavior only recently, then he probably has not yet developed a pattern. If the dog *has* had the problem for a long time, there is a good chance (or a bad one) that the dog has developed a behavior pattern. The longer the dog has been doing something like having accidents in the house, the more time it will take to get rid of the behavior.

It is important to understand that when this is the case, you have to *untrain* what the dog thinks is appropriate and teach him what is appropriate.

This leads us to my favorite word in problem-solving with dogs: *escalation*. The bad behavior *originates* from the first opportunity that an owner gave a dog, likely unintentionally, to engage in inappropriate behavior. The bad behavior happens once, then once a week, then a few times a week, and so on. If an owner has not been aware of it or has done nothing to try to stop it, the problem behavior can *escalate* into something that occurs every day. Remember that the longer the animal has had the problem, the more difficult it is to correct. This is why I always tell new owners to be aware of and be familiar with their dogs' behavior so they can notice a problem before it has the chance to escalate.

If your dog barks as "intruders" are leaving, he will just think that he's doing his job of protecting his home and family.

You also need to know that from the dog's point of view, the completion of the bad behavior is a reward in itself. Think about the following scenario: if your dog wants to get into the trash, and nobody is there to stop him, would he get into the trash? Yes. He doesn't know that the behavior is considered "bad" by his owners, but he knows that the trash can is full of enticing smells, so he wants to check it out. When he gets in there, will he find something to eat? Yes. And will he eat it? Yes. So getting into the trash will be quite a rewarding experience for your dog.

What about if your dog needs to relieve himself and there is nobody around to let him outside? If he relieves himself on the carpet, will he feel good afterward? Absolutely. Will he do it again? Absolutely.

If your dog barks at the mailman, it probably stemmed from a few days of barking at this unknown person in a uniform who approaches your house. If this person leaves each time (which he does) after the dog barks, the pattern develops. Over the course of time, the dog learns that if he barks, the person leaves, and he thinks that his barking is what causes the person to leave. Does this make your dog feel good? Absolutely. He was uncomfortable with the person in uniform, he barked, and the person left, resulting in a very rewarding experience for your dog. What's worse is that this behavior is reinforced six days a week.

The Color Chart

Different-colored dog require different training approaches. To recap, the color system is as follows:
Extremely high-strung dog: *Red*
Pretty high-strung dog: *Orange*
Average dog: *Yellow*
Pretty calm or shy dog: *Green*
Very calm or shy dog: *Blue*

Timing is a huge part of behavior modification. The last thing you want to do is reprimand your dog for actions that happened in the past—even just a few minutes in the past. An example is the owner that rubs his dog's nose in urine after the owner notices the wet spot on the carpet. Most dogs do not make the association between the past "accident" and the present punishment, so reprimanding your dog for a bad behavior that already occurred is a waste of time and could very likely jeopardize your dog's trust in you.

When you're problem-solving with your dog, you will work with a Blue, Green, or Yellow dog one way, and with an Orange or Red dog another way. The Orange and Red dogs are going to be a little more belligerent. If you are using physical corrections properly, they can work with Red and Orange dogs. One of my reasons for coming up with this color scheme is to teach owners that there are some dogs that should not receive physical corrections. With a mellow, shy, or timid dog, physical corrections are unnecessary. With the cool-colored dogs, physical corrections could emotionally damage them as well as damage their relationships with their owners.

Using a Chart

Take a look at the charts below. You will see that they each cover a fourteen-day period. On the blank chart, I want you to fill in the dates of the next two weeks along the bottom, starting with

Occurrences

4							
3	x	x	x	x			
2					x	x	
1							
0							
Date	Apr. 1	Apr. 2	Apr. 3	Apr. 4	Apr. 5	Apr. 6	

Occurrences

Date							

today's date at the left (or use the dates of whatever two-week period you want to chart). Take a look at the left side of the top chart; the numbers start from zero at the bottom and increase to four at the top. These numbers represent how many times an undesired behavior occurred each day. On the blank chart, you can use the same numbers, or you can fill in whatever numbers fit your dog's behavior problem. The idea of this chart is to document your dog's undesired behavior and to track your training progress. When you are having success, your check marks will move in a downward direction, as you can see in the example, to show the decrease in the unwanted behavior.

The example in the top chart represents a house-training problem that started on April 1. From April 1 to April 4, the dog was consistently having three accidents a day in the house. Then, for two days, he had only two accidents a day. He had a bit of a setback on April 7, after which he really started to show some improvement, because he had just one accident in the house each day for the next three days. He ended the two-week period with four straight accident-free days.

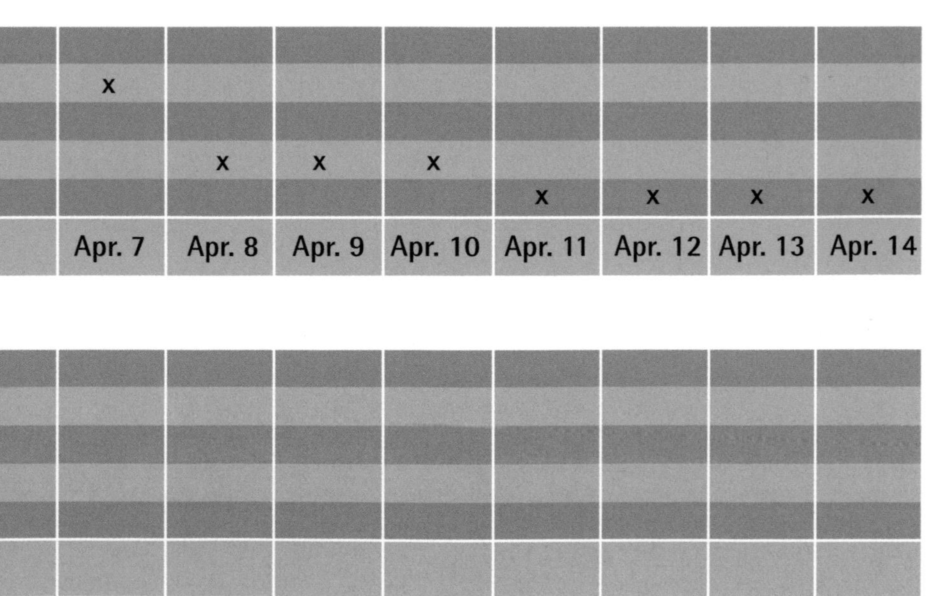

9

solving behavior problems

This chapter comprises some of the most common behavior problems that dog owners will encounter with new dogs. The first issue I talk about, running through a door or gate, should be one of your priorities if you have a dog with a yen to escape. You need to have control over your dog to keep him safe. The technique I show you for teaching your dog not to jump up on people is something that I teach in all of my classes and training DVDs, and it was the topic of one of my favorite *Good Dog U* episodes. I talk about barking and resource guarding, which can both be precursors to a dog's becoming possessive or aggressive. I will help you deal with these issues the best I can, but if the dog has already developed aggressive tendencies, you may need to bring in a professional trainer to work with your dog. I also talk about separation anxiety, which is seen rather frequently, as many owners must be away from home for work and other commitments. You will be using one of or a combination of three training methods—preventative training, corrections, and redirection—in working with your dog on these problems.

Running through the Door or Gate

In dealing with a dog who wants to dash out the door or backyard gate, you have to look at the behavior from the dog's point of view. In most cases, when you see dog about to make his escape, his ears are up as he crosses that threshold, and boy is he feeling good! This is a very reinforcing (self-rewarding) behavior for him. The reinforcement could come from a variety of things: attention from some neighbors he wants to see, interaction with the dog next door, or simply the opportunity to run. For whatever reason, we need to send a clear message to the dog that this behavior is not only unacceptable but also incredibly unsafe. There are two types of training techniques we are going to use to get rid of this behavior: physical correction and preventative training, the latter of which we've already discussed.

PHYSICAL CORRECTION

Before you train your dog to stay on the safe side of the door or gate, it is essential for him to know the *come* cue and how to respond to it reliably. If your dog does not know how to come to you when called, you'll need to teach him step by step with the following method.

Training Your Dog to Come

The great thing about training your dog to come is that you've already built the foundation for it by developing a good relationship with your dog. If your dog naturally wants to be with you, teaching him how to come when called should be fairly easy.

People who haven't taken the necessary time to build a positive relationship with their pets will find teaching the *come* behavior much more difficult. If your dog doesn't have solid trust in you, and you put him in a situation in which training becomes negative, such as calling him to you to scold him for something, the last thing he will want to do is come to you when you call him. A bond of love and trust makes all the difference in training.

Before you start teaching the dog to come, invest in a 30-foot line. You can find this very important tool at your favorite pet-supply shop. If you have a dog who weighs less than 30 pounds, you might need to use a lightweight version of this long leash.

There are many reasons for using a long line. Remember that most dogs who will not come when called know that their owners have no control over them. This is not necessarily due to the dog's being off leash; rather, the dog understands that once he is a certain distance from you, he does not have to come back to you when called. He simply has learned over time that the farther he is from you, the less control you have over him. In using the technique I am about to show you, you will be sending a clear message to your dog that no matter where or how far away he is in relation to you, he must come when you call him. Please read this very carefully before you take your dog outside:

1. **Go to an area where there are no distractions.**
2. **Attach the line to your dog's chain collar or regular collar.**
3. **Hold the line at about its halfway point.**
4. **Let the dog begin to sniff around and roam in whatever direction he chooses.**
5. **When the dog is 8 to 15 feet from you, say his name, followed by "Come" in a cheerful, happy voice. A happy tone of voice is very important. Say "Come" only once.**

The long line allows you to stay in control while working on the *come* cue with your dog at varying distances.

6. Give a light, quick correction (tug) with the leash if he doesn't respond to you within the first few seconds; this should cause him to come to you.
7. When he gets to you, use the leash to guide him right in front of you. It doesn't matter if he sits or stands. All that matters is that he stays in one place, pays attention to you, and does not wander off.
8. Give him a nice tactile reward. Early on in training this behavior, I will often kneel down and spend a good twenty to thirty seconds rewarding the dog with petting.

TOP: Start by letting the line out only about halfway. BOTTOM: When the dog is consistent at half the line's distance, start letting the line out a little more each time you repeat the exercise.

Coming to you must always result in something positive for the dog; that's how you get him to want to respond to your call every time.

Tips for Teaching *Come*

- If your dog ignores you and does not respond to the correction (leash tug), you may need to tug on the leash a little harder. The important thing is to always follow up with Step 7 from the foregoing list.
- It can be very helpful to run backward as the dog is coming toward you, because that will hasten the dog's pace and make you seem more exciting to him. He will be more likely to come running with enthusiasm. Alternatively, crouching down as you call the dog will also make coming to you more appealing to him.
- Encouraging your dog with "Good boy!" as he comes to you and using a happy voice will make you even more fun to approach.
- A mistake that owners make is to call the dog simply by using the dog's name– "Rover, Rover, Rover" –without telling Rover what they want. Calling a dog with "Rover, come!" puts a word to the cue, letting the dog know what is expected of him when he hears that word.

Using the Long Line

No matter what type of control you think you have early on, use the long line for at least a week. A mistake that many dog owners make is to fall into a false sense of security, thinking that the dog understands what they want, when in reality the animal still is learning. The last thing you want when training this behavior is to call the dog and have him not come to you.

Shaping the Behavior

We want the dog to understand that it really doesn't matter whether he is 3 feet away or 20 feet away. If he does not come when you call him, he will be corrected. Once your dog starts to consistently come to you from 8 to 15 feet away, start letting out more of the line each time you release him. Let it go 20 to 25 feet, call your dog, and see how he responds. If he comes to you after you call him just once, you are making great progress!

Once you correct your dog a few times, you may notice that he will stay closer to you and won't wander away. This is a good thing because it indicates that the dog is beginning to understand what you want. In that situation, you might even need someone to help you by distracting the dog so you can put some distance between you and the dog to practice the *come* exercise. When your dog is consistently coming to you on the long line, the next step is to replace the long line with the dog's regular leash and just let the leash drag. Do not remove the leash until your dog is reliably coming to you when called and you feel that you have control. Whether in training or in real-life situations, always take the time to give your dog a nice tactile reward when he comes to you.

Setting Up Scenarios

Now that your dog is trained to come, you can set up a scenario to mimic the behavior with which you're having trouble, such as the dog's running out the front door or the backyard gate. Attach the long line to your dog, take him to the problem area, and proceed with the following steps:

- **As your dog is attached to the long line, just let it drag.**
- **Have someone open the door or the gate.**
- **Let your dog go to the door or the gate as long line drags.**

- **Once your dog crosses the threshold, immediately say the dog's name and "Come!"**
- **If the dog comes to you without your having to touch the long line, give him a nice tactile reward.**
- **If the dog keeps going and ignores you, pick up the long line and give a leash correction, the same way you did when you were training the *come* behavior.**

"Can I succeed and run out the front door or the gate?" or *"Do I not run out the front door or the gate because I know I will be corrected?"* The animal will always make his own decision based on past experiences and consequences, good and bad, in these training sessions. Giving the dog the tools, through corrections for improper behavior and rewards for correct behavior, is what a good trainer will instill

TOP: Give the *come* cue at the moment that the dog crosses the threshold. BOTTOM: If he doesn't respond right away to your verbal cue, the leash tug should turn the dog around and bring him back to you.

As you did when teaching the dog to come, reward him with petting when he gets to you.

in the animal, and as far as I am concerned, it really is what animal training is all about.

What you are going to find is that most dogs just need a little direction. Sometimes all they need is a few corrections paired with the word *no* to understand what you want. As your dog begins to understand, you want to start fading out the physical correction of grabbing the leash and increasing your use of the word "No." This word will have meaning to him because you started by backing it up with that physical correction.

Soon the dog will start to understand that if he tries to run out the door or through the gate, he will be corrected. This is normally when I switch from the 30-foot line in training to the dog's normal 6-foot leash, the one used for walking him.

Let the 6-foot leash do what the long line was doing—just let it drag. It will feel the same to the dog as the 30-foot line did. In his mind, the dog knows that if the door or the gate is open, he cannot run out because you will grab the leash and correct him. Another very valuable message has now been sent to your dog.

Over the course of time, your dog will no longer even try to cross the threshold of the door or the gate, or in cases when he does try, a

TOP: The hope is that your "No" will be sufficient, and the dog will come back without your ever touching the leash. BOTTOM: The dog will want to return to you if you consistently greet him happily and with a reward.

simple "No" will be the only correction needed to deter him. When he responds by returning to you every time you say "No," this is when you'll know that it's safe to take off the leash.

The most important part of this training is not to rush it and take off the leash too early. If the leash is removed too soon, the dog will begin to discriminate between times when the leash is on and times when the leash is off, and he might start running out the door when he does not have the leash on. Just take it slow.

If you don't have the control to get him back, he will learn that he doesn't have to come to you when you call him. *If the dog thinks that coming to you is optional, you will have a real struggle in teaching him to be consistent in this behavior.* By taking the leash off too early, you can set yourself and your dog up for major problems down the road.

PREVENTATIVE TRAINING

To use preventative methods with a dog who wants to run out the door or escape through the gate, you need to make sure that everyone in the household is on the same page about the dog's training. This means that people need to be aware of where the dog is when they are leaving the house or yard and make sure that they do not give the dog the opportunity to run out.

Remember that the dog wants to run because it makes him feel good—you consider it a bad behavior, but he considers it rewarding. Again, if the door or the gate is open, *the dog is going to run*; the key to preventative training is to make sure that the dog never gets the chance to do so. It's important that the dog never be left loose in the house when a door is going to be opened. The same thing should apply with the gate in the backyard. If you're leaving the house, make sure that your dog is in his crate or in another room or that someone is holding on to him before you open the door. If you're leaving the yard and someone else is with you, have that person hold on to the dog as you open the gate.

Again, everyone in the household must be consistent. If one person lets the dog run out the door with him and the others are trying hard to prevent the dog from running, the dog will be confused. Any efforts to train the dog will be a waste of time if he thinks it's OK to run out the door at certain times. The purpose of preventative training is to prevent the dog from ever developing the bad behavior or to extinguish the bad behavior by never putting the animal in a situation where the behavior can occur.

Jumping Up

A common problem is a dog who jumps up on guests to his owners' home. The good news is that most dogs will do this only out of sheer excitement and will calm down after a few minutes, once the excitement of the arrival is over. However, this is not polite behavior and not the way that most guests want to be greeted. The great part about training this behavior is that once it's learned at the front door, you can use the same technique in other parts of the house to keep your dog from jumping up on counters, coffee tables, and other pieces of furniture.

Even if you enjoy a dog's effusive greeting, jumping up is not a behavior that should be encouraged.

With any behavior problem, you need to see if there is a chain of events that might *escalate* the dog's excitement level and make him even more out of control than he already is. This way, you can be aware of behavior patterns as they start to develop. Let's start with your dog jumping on guests when they enter the house. In trying to understand this behavior, you need to know what's going on in your dog's head. There is almost always the same behavior pattern—the same *escalation*—that happens prior to the dog's jumping on guests. Here is an example:

- **The dog hears the guest approaching the door, usually long before you do. This gets your dog excited.**
- **The guest knocks on the door or rings the doorbell. This sound gets your dog even more excited, and he will probably run to the door and possibly begin to bark.**
- **Now very excited, the dog puts his feet on the door. This action creates even more excitement.**
- **You open the door, and your dog sees the guest. The final result is the dog's jumping and possibly barking because he wants to get as close as he can to the guest.**

You can see where the dog's energy comes from as you look at how the excitement builds—*escalates*—and why this is one of the most common behavior problems in dogs. However, I have helped thousands of owners get rid of it. Remember, the completion of a behavior is always a reward in itself; in the case of jumping up, the dog is able to fulfill his desire to get as close to the person as he can. To extinguish the behavior, we will focus on two types of training:

- ***Correction training*, in which we teach the dog that if he is in the house when guests come over, he will always be wearing a leash and be corrected for jumping on guests.**
- ***Preventative training*, in which we are no longer going to give the dog the opportunity to be loose in the house when a guest comes through the door, thus preventing the dog from achieving the behavior.**

CORRECTION TRAINING

When you give your a dog a physical correction, it's very important to send a clear message to the dog so that you show him exactly what he is being corrected for. The only way to do that is if you understand why you are correcting the dog. *Once you understand, so will he.* In some cases, trainers will tell you to correct your dog for putting his feet up on the guest. *That's great, but it's a little too late.* You want to correct the dog for the *thought* of jumping up. When you taught your dog to stop running out the door, there was an exact moment when he was corrected—when he entered the threshold of the door. With jumping up, there is a thought that goes through your dog's brain that makes him want to put his feet up on the guest. The exact time to correct him is *just as he raises his feet off the ground.*

To teach your dog to not jump on guests, you need to set up a situation in which a guest opens the door. With a Red or Orange dog, keep a leash and chain collar next to the front door. For a Yellow, Green, or Blue dog, keep just a leash next to the front door, as you will simply use the collar that the dog is wearing. The scenario works as follows:

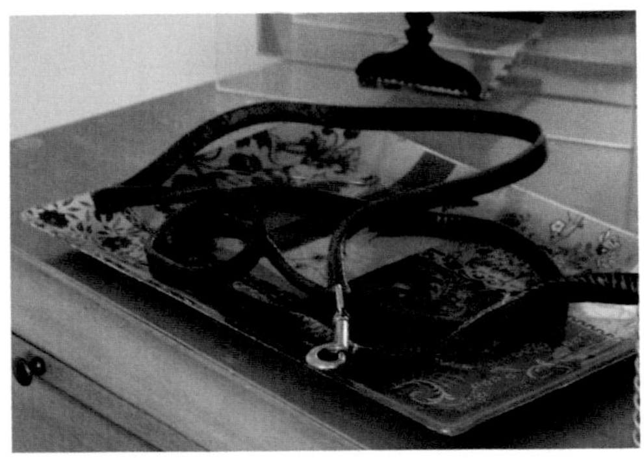

Have your leash by the door so you can put it on the dog quickly whenever a guest arrives.

1. **Have the guest knock on the door or ring the doorbell, whichever gets your dog the most excited. Your dog will likely start to bark and run to the door.**
2. **As you get to the door, pick up the leash or the leash and chain collar. Either snap on the leash or put the chain collar on the dog and attach the leash to the collar.**
3. **Have the guest open the door and walk a few feet into the house. At this time, your dog will be very excited.**
4. **When your dog's front feet lift off the ground as he starts to jump up, give a tug on the leash (physical correction), saying "No"** ***only once*** **at the same time. He may try to put his feet up again, and you may have to correct him again. Just make sure that you say "No" as you do it.**
5. **When the dog stops jumping and just stands there, have the guest pet him.**

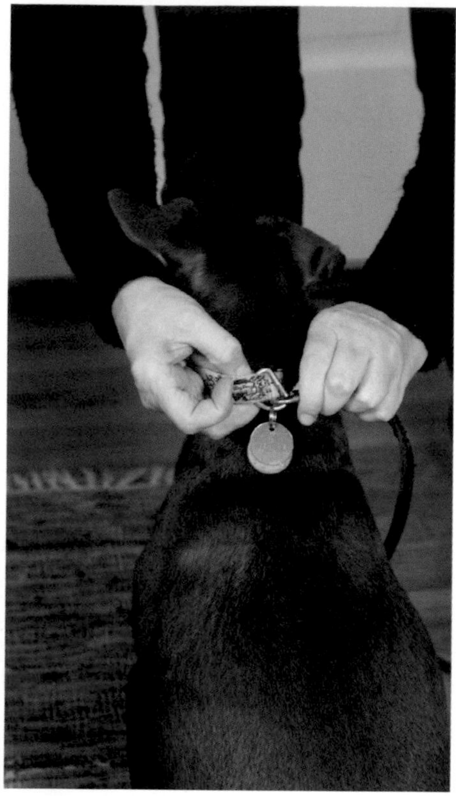

LEFT: Depending on your dog, you may use his regular buckle collar for training. RIGHT: Have your dog on leash before you open the door so that you're always in control.

Not only are you giving a physical correction and saying "No" to show the dog what he shouldn't be doing but you are also teaching the dog that he is rewarded for not jumping on the guest. What is nice about the correction is that is *not* coming from the guest. It is coming from a neutral place—behind the dog—from you. Most dogs will start to mellow out a few minutes after a guest enters the home. When you notice that your dog is calm, you can take off the leash (and chain collar, if you used one). Keep it in the same spot by the door so that you are always ready to use it.

Repeat this process for the first few training sessions. I recommend that you do three very short sessions a day, with two or three scenarios within each session. The sessions do not have to be long; many times, it takes only a few minutes to get the point across.

Correcting the dog after he's already jumped up is too late. Time your correction properly and never let the dog's front feet leave the ground.

After the second or third day, you are going to find that you don't have to correct your dog as firmly, or possibly not at all. You may also notice that "No" is beginning to have an impact on its own, without the physical correction. When you get to the point at which your dog responds to "No" and is no longer jumping on guests, you are ready to fade out the use of the leash. This means that when someone comes over, you will put only the chain collar on your dog or use his regular collar.

You can repeat the same process as you did with the leash, using just your hand on the collar to give a correction if needed. What's great about this is that it gives the dog the idea that you still have control; the only difference is that there is no leash. If you've been working with a chain collar, I suggest using it for four or five days, after which the behavior will be trained, and you can fade out the chain collar. Otherwise, simply use the dog's regular collar.

PREVENTATIVE TRAINING

The preventative way to address jumping up is to practice and enforce a *sit-stay* (discussed in Chapter 10) with your dog when someone comes to the door. If you first build your dog up to a three-minute sit-stay without distractions, you can then build him up to a three-minute sit-stay with the distraction of someone coming into your home or approaching your dog anywhere.

Barking

I want to make it clear that here I am discussing a *barking* problem only, not an *aggression* or *resource-guarding* problem. If you feel that your dog's problem is more than just barking, I suggest that you read the information on resource guarding later in the chapter or bring in a professional who deals specifically with aggression.

Here are some of the common situations in which dogs engage in problem barking:

- **When he's looking out the window at people**
- **When a person knocks on the door or rings the doorbell**
- **When a person enters the house**
- **When he's on a leash**
- **When he's in the backyard when you are home**
- **When he's in the backyard when you are not home**

We will be using a combination of correction and redirection to help you deal with your dog's barking problem based on his personality.

A dog may think of barking as part of his "job"—sounding the alarm to alert his family to anything out of the ordinary.

STEP 1—THE SCENARIO

If you have more than one dog, see if you can identify a specific dog who instigates the problem barking. If one dog in particular gets the other dogs going, you may have to train only that one dog not to bark. For simplicity of explanation, I'll outline the steps for training one dog. Once you have identified the dog who gets the barking going, ask yourself these questions:

- **Does the barking happen only in the house? If not, where else does it occur?**
- **Does the barking happen only in the backyard or in other places outdoors?**
- **Are there certain times when the dog barks more often?**
- **Is the barking directed only toward people?**
- **Is the barking directed only at stationary objects or only at moving objects?**

The place where your dog does most of his barking is where you will train him. You will set up a scenario in which the dog is going to want to bark. Remember that, like a child, your dog does not know that he is doing something wrong unless you teach him. What you are going to do is get the dog to bark and then correct him for the barking. Once that happens, the dog begins to understand that his behavior is wrong and why he is being corrected.

If your dog is barking at people out the window, start training by having a person stand at a distance from the house. Remember that the closer the person is to the window, the more excited the dog will become, so don't start out with the person standing right next to the window. If you correct the dog when he is in an agitated, overexcited state, the corrections are going to be more severe for the dog because he is so close to what is making him bark and thus acting out of control. We want the dog to be able to process what is happening.

I mention this because you want your corrections to be as small and as easy for the dog to understand as possible. The smaller and simpler the corrections are, the easier they are on your dog, and the simpler the training is for you. If you put a person right next to your window, your dog will probably bark relentlessly at the person. If the person stands on the sidewalk, though, the dog will still bark, but likely a lot less frantically, setting up a better training scenario for you and the dog.

STEP 2—USING A CORRECTION

Let's use the dog's barking out the window at someone as an example. As I just mentioned, we want to set up a scenario that results in an easy correction for you and the dog. The less the dog is barking, the more minimal will be your physical correction.

- **Make sure that your area by the window will be easy for you and your dog to work in. A suggestion for a small dog is to put him on the couch.**
- **For a small dog, a Blue dog, or a Green dog, I recommend attaching a leash to the regular collar. For Orange or Red dogs that are out of control, you may need to use a chain collar.**
- **Hold the leash about 4 to 6 inches from where it attaches to the collar.**
- **Start with your helper out of sight. When you are ready, have the person appear on the sidewalk. When the dog sees the person and starts barking, say "No" while giving a small tug on the leash. You want to be more annoying than anything else as you give the correction.**

Before you have the dog look out the window, attach his leash and get in a position that's comfortable for both of you.

- Repeat the correction as needed over the course of about thirty to forty-five seconds. What we're hoping for is that the dog will think to himself, "Wow, that is really irritating, and it happens every time I bark. Maybe I should stop barking and see if that's more pleasant."
- When the dog stops barking, have the person outside move out of the dog's sight.
- Repeat the exercise. If the dog barks. correct him. If the dog does not bark when the person appears, reward the dog and have the person remove himself from the dog's sight. End the session.
- Start the next session with the person in the same place as before.
- If the dog does not bark at the person, you are ready to have the person stand 25 percent closer to the window. Follow the same procedure of correcting the dog while saying "No" each time he barks.
- When you have success at this level, the next step is to get the person to stand 5 to 10 feet away from the window. Repeat the same procedure.
- The next step is to have the person stand next to the window. Follow the same procedure of correcting the dog for barking while you say "No."
- Once the dog is no longer barking at the person outside the window, have the person stand at the front door and knock very softly. At this point, bring the dog to the door on leash; this will give you the control you need. If the dog starts to bark, follow the same procedure as you did at the window.
- Once the dog is OK with this, you can have the person knock a little louder and start ringing the doorbell.
- When the dog is consistently quiet in this scenario, you can take the dog off leash when the person comes to the door.

STEP 3—USING REDIRECTION

Once your dog has stopped barking at the person, to make things more fun and interesting for the dog, we are going to start having the person give the dog some sort of high-value treat each time the person walks in the house and the dog *does not bark*. This is great, because now the dog will understand that not only is he not allowed to bark but also that he is being rewarded for not barking. Some owners may try to skip the correction step, thinking that redirection with a reward is the sole answer. In my opinion, when you are dealing with a barking problem, there must be a negative (correction) combined with a positive (redirection).

Resource Guarding

Resource guarding is when a dog becomes possessive over people, animals, objects (such as food or toys), or territory. A dog who resource-guards may not start off as an aggressive dog; on the other hand, you may see resource guarding in dogs who are already showing some signs of aggression. This is not something that is isolated to dogs who are prey-aggressive; some fear-aggressive dogs will resource-guard as well. It is essential that you recognize this behavior early. Resource guarding that goes unchecked over time and is allowed to escalate can blow up into major aggression problems, which we will discuss later in this chapter.

Resource guarding is displayed in a number of ways. Sometimes the animal may actually redirect his aggression away from the object

Food bowls are common objects of a dog's resource-guarding behavior.

or person of which he is possessive onto a different person or object. Because there are so many variables involved in understanding resource guarding, let's look at a few examples:

- **If a dog growls at people or other animals when he is eating or when an animal or person makes any move toward his food bowl, that behavior will most likely escalate into a more severe form of aggression, such as snapping or biting.**
- **If a dog is successful at bullying other animals around by growling and snarling, he will continue to do so, and there is a good chance that the dog will become more aggressive or resort to extreme behaviors such as biting.**
- **If every time a dog holds a bone in his mouth, his hackles (the fur on his shoulder blades) go up in a threatening stance, he will learn over time that he can get away with this display, and he will most likely begin to do other things, such as snarling and growling, as he gets even more possessive.**
- **If a dog becomes jealous over a specific person, and no one is there to redirect the dog, the behavior can continue to grow and escalate.**

Those are just a few examples, but you can see how the common thread in each is the animal's becoming more and more possessive.

One of the best ways to deal with resource guarding is to use *redirection*. The goal is to redirect the dog's focus from the object, person, or animal over which he is possessive to something else that is of *value* to the dog. This can work if there is a treat that is of high enough value for that particular dog.

Let me give you an example of how using a high-value treat can work with a dog who has become possessive of his owner. Let's imagine that there is an elderly woman living in her apartment with her little dog, and every time a new person walks into the apartment, this little dog begins to growl at the person. This behavior is not isolated to one person; it happens with every stranger. The owner needs to find a way to redirect the animal away from resource guarding.

Let's say that this dog has a strong food drive and particularly loves steak. In this case, the dog's owner would no longer give him steak; rather, he would receive bits of steak from strangers during thirty-second training sessions. Let's look at these sessions in detail; in the scenarios, you, the owner, are the one holding the dog's leash.

ABOVE: Start with the person at a distance from the dog, paying no attention to him. RIGHT: As you approach the person with the dog on leash, the person will not acknowledge the dog's arrival.

- Start off in a neutral place where the dog is less likely to become territorial—perhaps the front yard.
- Have your helper—the "stranger"—hold a small piece of steak in his hand.
- The person should be facing away from and looking away from the dog. The key is that this person should appear as a "prop" to the dog.
- Have the dog on a leash at a good, comfortable distance

away from the other person to start.

- **Walk the dog on leash to the person with the treat. When the dog gets to the person, the person will give the dog the steak and then walk away.**
- **Repeat the sequence thirty minutes later. On your first day of training, you'll repeat this sequence every few hours.**
- **Keep the sessions short, no more than thirty to forty-five seconds, to always leave the dog wanting more.**

Let me ask you a question: If we do this for a few days, do you think that the dog might become focused on the treat that the person is offering him instead of trying to "guard" you from the person? After only a few days, the resource-guarding behavior will be a long way from being extinguished, but you will see how *redirection* can start to work in a very positive way in a short time. Most importantly, you can see how we can build from here!

Next, have the person face the dog before the dog comes over to take the treat. The person should then kneel down and let the dog

The helper avoids eye contact with the dog and does not interact with him except to offer the treat.

take the treat, still avoiding most eye contact. After this step, have the person slowly walk toward the dog as you walk the dog toward the person. The person gives the dog the treat when they meet.

When the dog is comfortable with the person in the neutral area, you can then take the person to the front door, where you'll start over at the beginning of the sequence and work your way up. This means that you are going to walk your dog on leash to the person and let the dog take the treat from the person. The person is again facing away from the dog like he did at the beginning of your previous training sessions. You'll progress through the rest of the steps as the dog grows comfortable with each: the person facing the dog as the dog approaches for the treat, the person kneeling down and offering the treat, and, finally, the person walking toward the dog as the dog is walking toward the person, with the person giving the dog the treat when they meet.

By this time, you will most likely see a change in the dog's attitude toward the helper as he becomes more accepting of him

LEFT: As in your training exercises outdoors, the person faces away from the dog and does not make eye contact. RIGHT: Eventually you progress to where your helper can kneel down to offer treats.

As you succeed at each phase of training in different locations, the dog will begin to relax around your helper.

or her. Many times, as we start to redirect the animal, it actually becomes a game for the dog. With some working breeds or mixed-breed dogs who have fear of a person, this type of training actually gives them a job.

Once the dog is really focused on the person, the next step is to let the dog start to follow the person with the treat around the house. The person will give the dog a treat every ten to twenty seconds and vary the time between the treats. Keep each training session to one or two minutes, no longer. These scenarios offer just one example of how *redirection* can work; this behavior issue is a good one with which to try the redirection technique.

Separation Anxiety

Throughout this chapter, I've used the word *escalation* frequently. That's because in dealing with problem-solving issues, I have seen small behavior issues become full-blown problems when not addressed. Separation anxiety is one of the most common examples.

Many dogs have the potential to develop separation anxiety, which often originates in the animal's desire not to be left alone. This can happen in a dog who is very attached to a specific person or people. Separation anxiety is exhibited in different behaviors, and in varying degrees of severity. As with other behavior problems, if an owner catches separation anxiety early enough, he or she can work with the dog to extinguish the behavior before it escalates. If the behavior has gone unnoticed for a while, it could take a lot more time to rectify.

Separation anxiety can happen in dogs of all breeds, mixes, and sizes. It seems to be triggered by something that goes on in the dog's head when he is alone, and this can really increase the dog's anxiety. Understanding how a dog's anxiety escalates can help you understand and, most importantly, eliminate, the resulting behaviors.

If you were to watch a dog with separation anxiety when his owner leaves the house, you'd see the same chain of events each time. If a dog is left loose in the house or yard, he may start to pace right off the bat. As a matter of fact, he might start to walk or run in a certain pattern—maybe along the perimeter of a fence, back and forth in front of a screen door, or up and down the stairs—and that pattern is usually the same each time his owner leaves. Pacing is the animal's way of dealing with the stress of separation from his owner.

Here's where things start to change: as the animal becomes a little more stressed out, and things begin to escalate, the pacing can be coupled with whining or even barking, depending on the breed and personality of the dog. In extreme cases, the dog will whine or bark nonstop while his owner is gone.

Many dogs are left alone at home during working hours, anticipating their owners' return.

As the dog becomes still more stressed, he may start digging at the door, by the gate, near the window, or at the last place he saw his owner. It really doesn't matter if it's inside or outside. If he is in the house, he may choose the carpet, chairs, or couch to dig at and tear up. If the dog is in the backyard and he last saw his owner walking through the sliding screen door, he may start digging at the screen. Outside, he may also dig holes and uproot plants.

The problem will continue to worsen as the dog keeps digging, tearing things up, and even chewing to deal with his stress. Probably the most severe manifestation of separation anxiety is when the animal is so stressed out that he begins to lick and chew on himself.

Again, there are certainly different levels of this problem. The solution to dealing with separation anxiety is to eliminate the opportunity for it to escalate. There is no magic cure, and your probability of success and how long it will take you to achieve it really depend on the severity of the dog's separation anxiety.

I have successfully used *preventative training* in the form of *crate-training* to eliminate separation anxiety. We have to set a goal, and our goal is to not put the dog in a situation in which he will have a chance to become stressed out. At the same time, we will find things that the dog likes and that he can have when he's alone.

First, identify the place in your home where your dog is most comfortable. It might be a certain room or secluded area. As you identify the places that your dog likes, you should also be identifying places that your dog does not like or that make him uncomfortable. For example, it may make your dog uncomfortable to be given run of the entire house. We know for sure that dogs are *den animals*, which means, in general, that they are more comfortable in confined areas.

"P" is for Patience

"I'm so happy to see you, I could pee!" Even though it's not called *joyful* urination, it's the same thing, and it's a real problem for many dog owners. For the dogs, it's not just about joy, but also the excitement or sometimes scariness of saying hello, often to strangers, but sometimes to their owners.

With a rescue dog, the new owners don't always know about the rapport the dog had with his previous owners. We all know people who come home from work in foul moods. Similarly, a dog may expect his owner to come home at the end of the day and scold him for chewing on a table leg, messing on a carpet, or engaging in some other activity to relieve boredom, and he urinates as a reaction to the scolding (or the anticipation of being scolded).

Submissive urination is easy to recognize: the owner comes home from work or somewhere else, and the dog comes running to greet him or her, either urinating on the way or in front of his owner during the greeting. In the less joyful version, the dog doesn't even have to come running; he may simply walk slowly to the owner in a submissive posture and then begin urinating.

Dogs who wet in this way usually don't even know that they're peeing. It's not a house-training problem at all, and it can't really be considered a behavior problem, either. With that in mind, realize that you cannot correct a dog for submissive urination. If

Something that can provide this need for a den is a crate, which is why I highly recommend crate-training. If your dog is already crate-trained for house-training purposes, then you're one step ahead of the game. If your dog is not yet crate-trained, use the following method, which differs slightly from the method described in Chapter 4.

To begin training, put the crate in an area of the house in which your dog is comfortable, then scatter six or seven broken-up treats in the back of the crate. This way, the dog has to go all the way into the crate to get the treats. Leave the crate door open so the dog knows that he can eat the treats and come out of the crate. Allow the dog to go in, eat the treats, and exit the crate a few times, making this a very short training session.

the dog doesn't know he's done something, correction is worthless and can add to the problem.

Often, owners don't realize that their actions are part of the escalation of the problem. Here's some advice to prevent submissive urination: first, limit direct eye contact with the dog when you greet him. Whether the problem is actually a submission thing or not, facing away from the dog usually helps. Second, change your tone of voice. Don't greet the dog with your high-pitched "How's my good boy?" voice, which can excite the dog. Enter the house and be very matter of fact.

To use redirection, as soon as you open the door, immediately make a move to the back door and let the dog follow you outside. If you don't have a back door, you'll want to come inside with a leash in hand and methodically lead the dog outside. The idea is to not give the dog a chance to urinate by avoiding the indoor "I'm home" ritual altogether. Ideally, the dog will relieve himself outside. Once he's done so, you can greet him happily. This should help you condition your dog to not urinate indoors and upon greeting you. With patience and a little time, most dogs overcome this problem.

Lastly, if your perfectly house-trained pooch is peeing randomly when you greet him or now and then when you pet him, take him to the vet to check for a health problem. A simple urinary-tract infection can manifest itself in this exact behavior.

You want your dog to be calm and quiet in the crate.

After the third or fourth such training session, shut the door for about ten seconds while the dog is inside the crate, eating the treats. After the ten-second period, open the door and let the dog come out. It is essential at this stage that the dog never feels like he is trapped in the crate. Scatter more treats in the crate, but this time leave the crate door open so the dog can eat the treats and exit the crate when he wants. You want to be unpredictable so that the dog never knows if you are going to shut the door or leave it open.

Unlike with house-training, in which we would start shutting the door for thirty minutes at this point, you will start shutting the door for thirty seconds and then letting the dog out. After a few days of training the thirty-second intervals, close the crate door when the dog goes in, then walk away from the crate and go into another room for about a minute.

Take note of your dog's reactions. If the dog does not bark or make any other noise, such as whining, let him out after a minute. If he does make noise, do not let him out; if you do, he will learn that you will let him out for barking or whining. Wait it out until he is quiet. This is especially important in the early stages of crate-training.

The next step is to repeat what you did in the previous training session (shutting the door for a thirty-second interval), but this time put the dog in the crate for about three minutes with you out of the room. If everything is OK, open the door and let the dog out.

For two days, repeat this short training session three times a day. In some of those sessions, put the dog in the crate, shut the door, and open it about *five seconds* later. Here again, you will be unpredictable so that the dog never knows for how long he will be in the crate. This is essential for training a dog with separation anxiety.

For the next two days, increase the amount of time your dog is in the crate to ten to fifteen minutes at a time. For one session each day, put the dog in the crate, shut the door, and open it about five seconds later. Repeat the process over the next two days, this time keeping the dog in the crate for twenty minutes at a time except for the one daily session in which you'll open the door after five seconds. Over the course of the next two days, increase your dog's crate time to thirty minutes at a time. When your dog is comfortable being in the crate for thirty minutes with no barking, whining, or digging at the crate, you will know you're making great progress.

The next step is to repeat what you just did, but walk out the door and remain on the front porch with the front door closed. Start with thirty seconds and progress from there. As you did in the previous phase of training, have one session per day in which you put the dog in the crate, leave, and then immediately come back in to let him out. As your dog becomes more conditioned to being in the crate, you will eliminate this step. You can see how much slower the crate-training process is for separation anxiety compared with the timetable for crate-training for house-training.

Don't forget that dogs are den animals, and although the dog may not initially want to be away from you, he will get used to the crate over time. A crate-trained dog will not have the opportunity to start the process of anxiety-related behaviors. When the dog is in a crate, he doesn't get the chance to start pacing—it's impossible. If he does not get a chance to pace, his behavior will not escalate to barking, and thus will not escalate from barking to digging and chewing.

While crate-training can be successful in eliminating separation anxiety and its related behavior problems, there are no absolute cures. Some dogs get so nervous and so neurotic when alone that they need medication.

Keep in Mind

Here are just a few points to remember as you go about dealing with some of the problems you may face with your new best friend in a safe, easy, and humane way:

- **All dogs come with baggage, just as people do. Some have more than others.**
- **As much as some owners may want to, they will never find the "perfect" dog.**
- **A dog cannot read your mind, and sometimes all he needs is a little direction.**

10 teaching sit and stay

In this chapter, I will be helping you train your dog to sit and to stay. There are two ways I train the dog to sit: by *using treats* and with *gentle manipulation*. I recommend using treats, if possible. However, there are some dogs who get so out of control with treats that the owners have much better luck using gentle manipulation and rewarding the dog with petting. Gentle manipulation is often necessary with Red and Orange dogs, but you should be able to use treats to train a Yellow, Green, or Blue dog to sit. The *stay* is taught the same way for dogs of every color.

There are a few points to keep in mind:

- **Keep the sessions short—two to five minutes at a time.**
- **Have an easy, attainable goal for the training session in mind before you start. When you achieve that goal, end the session. You want to end every session on a positive note.**
- **After you end the training session, do something fun that your dog likes—it might be playing with his favorite toy, throwing a ball for him, giving him a treat, taking him for a walk, or just petting him. Doing something like this with you makes training even more rewarding for your dog. If you dog has fun after each training session, he will come to understand that the less time it takes him to do what you want, the sooner he will get his reward.**
- **It is very important that when you give your dog the *cue* (command), you say it *only one time*. Many owners have communication problems with their dogs because they give *multiple cues.* For example, the owner says "Sit, sit, sit" instead of just "Sit" before manipulating the dog into position.**
- **When your dog does something incorrectly, always use the same correction. Change in itself is reinforcing, so if you vary corrections, your dog may perceive them as rewards instead.**

Blue, Green, and Yellow Dogs: *Sit/Stay* Using Treats

Before getting started, you should prepare your training area. I recommend placing the dog on an elevated surface when training the *sit*. You'll find that is easier and much more relaxing for your dog—and a lot kinder to your back. For a smaller dog, this could be a sturdy table, a couch, or a chair; for a larger dog, this could be something as little as 5 or 6 inches higher than the surface on which you are standing, like a low porch. As we begin to train, you will see why we do this.

Start training in an area that is comfortable for the dog and has as few distractions as possible. If he's comfortable being in the backyard, that would be a great place to start. Even if you're indoors or in an enclosed area outdoors, be sure to have your dog on a leash.

By now, you've found some type of treat that your dog particularly likes. For training, keep the treats somewhere accessible to you but inaccessible to your dog. I recommend wearing a little pouch or fanny pack during training to hold the treats.

An elevated surface gives you a defined area that your dog will learn to associate with training.

PHASE 1

In this phase, you use a treat to get the dog to sit and start teaching him the hand signals for the *sit* and *stay* cues.

1. **Get the dog on the training area so that he is simply standing on all fours, facing you. Initially, you want to make the dog feel relaxed, simply by petting him. This might take a few minutes.**

Combining the *Sit* and the *Stay*

I always like to train the *sit* and *stay* behaviors at the same time. If your dog understands that he is to stay each time he is told to sit, you end up with an incredible amount of control early on, which makes training other behaviors much easier.

I also like to train these two behaviors first because they are the simplest for the dog to understand. It is nearly impossible for the dog to "cheat" with these behaviors, as he has to get up to break the *sit/stay* position.

TOP: Begin by showing your dog the treat to motivate him and direct his attention onto you. BOTTOM: Once the dog knows that you're holding a treat, he should focus on your hand.

2. Take out a treat and give it to the dog. Very simple! After you give it to him, just pet him, creating a positive association with your training area. Don't rush this step; repeat it a few times if needed. You can also talk to the dog to help him relax. You want him feeling comfortable just taking the treat from your hand.
3. Next, holding the leash *lightly* with your left hand, place a treat between the thumb and index finger of your right hand so the dog can see it.
4. Hold the treat 2 or 3 inches over your dog's head. Move it very slowly back, toward his tail, keeping the treat at the same height and saying "Sit" once.
5. For your dog to keep his eye on the treat as you move it toward his tail, one of two things must happen: he must jump for it, or he must sit as his head looks up and back.
6. As soon as your dog sits, reward him right away.

The farther your hand goes back, the farther the dog's rear must go down for him to maintain his balance until eventually he ends up in the *sit* position, at which point he gets the treat.

7. Immediately say "Stay" and hold your right hand in the air; this is the visual cue for the *stay*. If he stays, reward him with the treat, then release him with a word such as "OK" and give him lots and lots of praise. The mark of a good trainer is timing. You always want to make sure that the dog is rewarded immediately after he completes a behavior that you asked for.
8. Repeat the entire process three or four times, making sure that you say "Sit" only one time as you hold the treat over the dog's head and start moving it toward his tail. As soon as he sits, remember to say "Stay" and then reward your dog. Afterward, give the release cue.
9. When the dog is performing with some consistency, end the session and do something fun with your dog.
10. When your dog is consistent from one training session to the next—meaning that he assumes the *sit* position every time you move the treat toward his tail—you can move on to the next phase.

PHASE 2

In this phase, you will fade out the use of the treat. Using the same motions, but without the treat in your hand, you will teach the dog to eventually respond to visual (hand) and verbal signals alone.

1. **You're going to start fading out the action of moving the treat toward the dog's tail. Instead of moving the treat, just hold it stationary over the dog's head and say "Sit,"** ***looking*** **like you're going to move the treat back over his head. When the dog sits, say "Stay" and reward the dog immediately. Your dog now understands that when you hold a treat**

ABOVE and ABOVE, RIGHT: The dog has learned to associate your hand movements with the *sit* cue and will follow your hand even when you're not holding a treat. RIGHT: After rewarding the dog for the *sit*, immediately give the verbal and visual cues for *stay*.

over his head and say "Sit," he sits. Make sure that your dog is very consistent with this before moving on to the next step.

2. You are now going to start fading out the use of treats. Hold your hand, without a treat, in the same starting position over your dog's head and say "Sit." It looks just like you are still holding the treat, doesn't it? Your hand placement will become the dog's visual cue to sit. If he sits, tell him to stay and reward him.
3. You're now giving your dog the visual and verbal cues to sit. If he does so consistently, *congratulations!* You've just trained your dog to sit.

Using the Leash for Corrections

Remember that you are holding the leash in the hand without the food. You want to have a little slack in the leash, keeping the hand with the leash lower than your dog's head. As you hold the treat over your dog's head with the other hand, you will be able to control your dog with the leash and keep him from jumping up. When he tries to jump for the treat, he won't be able to get off the ground. There is no real physical correction because your dog never gets the opportunity to jump. After trying a few times and realizing that he can't get the treat by jumping, he should sit. Just make sure that you always have slack in the leash.

Orange and Red Dogs: *Sit/Stay* Using Gentle Manipulation

Again, this technique is for dogs who are so out of control that treats just make them even more high-strung. Before you start training your Red or Orange dog to sit and stay, I recommend doing a simple exercise with him. This exercise teaches your dog a little control and helps you get comfortable working with the leash and chain collar.

PRE-TRAINING FOR REDS AND ORANGES

I've emphasized in previous chapters the importance of properly putting a chain collar on your dog. It's important for you to understand that the right way to use the chain collar so you can administer an effective and fair correction.

Many dog owners make the mistake of letting the dog wander several feet away before they actually correct him. They might even let the dog lunge ahead before they correct him. Letting the dog get ahead of you and not correcting him right away sends mixed messages, and mixed messages can encourage behavior problems to develop. First of all, if the dog is allowed to get this far away from you before you correct him, will he understand why he is being corrected? Second, there are some people who simply do not have the strength to give an effective correction from such a distance. Going through the following steps will teach you how to send the right message to your dog by correcting him in the proper manner.

Start out with the dog standing at your left side and with a slack leash.

1. **Attach the leash to the chain collar as previously described.**
2. **Put your dog on your left side, facing in the same direction as you are, as if you're about to walk with him. It doesn't matter if the dog sits or stands as long as he's next to you, at your left side, in a stationary position. It is very important to keep the dog's nose either right behind, next to, or a few inches in front of your leg.**
3. **Keep slack in the leash.**
4. **If the dog starts to lunge away from you or pull, correct him right away**

with a small tug on the leash. Because you are so close to the dog, it will be a very light, minimal correction; remember, the closer the dog is, the easier the correction is on both of you. You do not need to say "No." Let the chain collar do the talking.

5. After you correct the dog, pet him very gently and talk to him in a soft tone.

From Manipulation to Treats

If you are training a high-strung dog, such as an Orange, to sit, you want to start the training using gentle manipulation. As the training progresses, the dog will move toward the center of the color spectrum. Your Orange dog, for example, will become more Yellow; once this happens and he seems calm enough to take a treat from you, you can switch to training with treats.

It is very important to understand that most Red dogs want attention. The dog is learning that if he sits or stands next to you and is relaxed, he will be rewarded with petting. At the same time, if he makes any movement out of position, he will be corrected. What we are creating is an attitude. This is such an important part of Red-dog training, because it sends a clear and distinct message of what you expect from the beginning. By going through this pre-training exercise, you've made training simpler for your dog. The dog will easily understand that in order to receive the petting or tactile rewards, he must stay in control next to you and, most importantly, not be pulling.

This is a critical exercise to do before you begin training, so be sure to take your time with it—even a few extra days, if needed. Practice until your dog is consistently staying next to your left side without pulling on the leash before moving on to training your dog to sit and stay. Remember that all dogs are different, and some will need a little more time than others.

Additionally, and very importantly, you've learned the right way to put a chain collar on your dog and how to use it properly to correct him. You've learned that you don't have to yank on the collar to deliver an effective correction. In doing so, you've made things easier on yourself and on your dog. This technique lays a great foundation for all of the behaviors and problem-solving techniques discussed in this book.

If you were to do what many dog owners do and just put a leash and a chain collar on an out-of-control dog and start trying to teach him to sit, you can imagine some of the problems you would have. If this dog had a serious lunging or jumping problem, how difficult would it be to teach any new behavior, let alone simply keeping him under control?

PHASE 1

In this phase, you will learn how to guide the dog into the *sit* position and teach him to stay there. Find a training area with something on which you can elevate your dog, such as a porch, a step, a table, or even a curb. I will discuss why we do this later in the chapter. Make sure that your dog is on leash.

1. **Guide your dog up onto the elevated area. Once he's up there, give him tactile reinforcement with petting. He should be a little calmer on the leash since you spent a few days doing the pre-training exercise with him.**
2. **Once he is facing you and in control, drop the leash. If the dog jumps off the elevated area at any time, grab the leash and guide the dog back into place. This will teach him from the start that the training area is where he needs to stay.**
3. **When you are happy with the dog's position, and he is calm, put one hand**

Holding the Leash

Many dog owners are unaware of the importance of a slack lead. It makes a huge difference in the potential success of a training exercise. Having *no* slack in the leash is not good; because there is continuous pressure on the leash, the dog will only learn to pull and *pull harder*. He will never learn to just stand or sit there, and he will become conditioned to the constant tugging on the leash.

You always want to keep some slack in the leash. When you get to the point where the dog sits or stands next to you on his own *with* slack in the leash, you will know you've made progress.

on his chest. Talk to the dog softly as you do this. Put the other hand on the dog's rear end, at the base of his tail.

4. When you feel like you have some control, say "Sit" and start to manipulate the dog's position by applying downward pressure with your hand at the base of his tail. At the same time, apply backward pressure with your hand on his chest. Both hands moving together create a type of backward "rocking" motion.
5. Reward the dog as soon as he sits.
6. Immediately say "Stay," holding your hand in the air with your palm facing the dog.
7. If the dog stays for a few seconds, reward him right away using a tactile reward.
8. Release him with "OK" and let him get up.

When you look back at the sequence of events, take good look at steps 6 and 7. A major mistake that many owners make is not teaching the dog to stay at this point in the training. Think about it from

TOP: Take a moment to make sure that the dog is calm and relaxed in the training area. BOTTOM: Notice the position of the hands on the dog's chest and rear.

TOP: As one hand guides the dog's chest up, the other hand guides the dog's rear down. BOTTOM: With your gentle hands-on guidance, the dog ends up sitting.

your dog's point of view. If he is not told to stay, he will probably get up on his own, taking control of the session. The last thing you want to do early on in training is lose control. By teaching your dog to stay right from the start, you gain control.

To summarize, the sequence of events is:

- **Say "Sit."**
- **Gently manipulate the dog into the sitting position.**
- **Reward for the sit and immediately say "Stay."**
- **Reward the dog.**
- **Release the dog.**

PHASE 2

At this point, you will start fading out the gentle manipulation so that your dog eventually responds to only your verbal and visual (hand) cues. If you now feel that you do not need to keep a hand on your dog's chest and manipulate him as much, it means that he's starting to understand what you want. Soon you will barely have to touch his back area as you say "Sit," and he will sit. Remember to say "Stay," reward him, and release him as you have always done.

The hand signal used with the gentle manipulation method is a little different than the hand signal used with treats.

You are soon going to find that just as you go to touch your dog and say "Sit," he sits. That's great, because he sat before you touched him. Immediately reward him for doing so.

The initial hand cue for *sit* looks very much like your hand when it is guiding the dog's rear into the *sit* position. Once your dog is taking the cue from a few inches away consistently, he will probably respond when your hand is a little farther—as much as 6 inches to a foot—away as you say "Sit."

Issue the visual cue (hand signal) for *stay* once you've rewarded the dog for sitting. This step is the same in the treat-based method.

Reinforcing the *Stay* for Dogs of All Colors

Many new dog owners have trouble getting their dogs to stay. There's a common reason for this. The dog sits right away and things appear to be going well, but when the owner says "Stay" and the dog stays for a moment, the owner then calls the dog to him before rewarding the dog.

Think about this from your dog's point of view. Remember that your dog naturally wants to come to you and be with you. By calling him to you to reward him for sitting and staying, you are making the come-to-me doubly rewarding—so why would your dog ever want to stay? Additionally, you're actually rewarding the *come* behavior rather than the *sit* and *stay*. To reward the *sit* and *stay*, your dog needs to be rewarded in the exact place where he is staying. You need to consistently *walk to your dog* and reward him.

Troubleshooting

Did you have a problem somewhere in the training process? For example, did your dog get right up after he sat, or did he jump off the training area? It's OK—I'm here to help. First, remember not to make a big deal out of it if your dog makes a mistake. Here are some things that you *do not* want to do:

- Say "No."
- Yell at your dog.
- Yank on your dog's leash.
- Hit your dog.

A trademark of my technique is to deal with mistakes by quietly guiding the dog back to doing what you want him to do. If your dog steps off the elevated area, just use the leash to bring him back to the spot, then repeat the behavior that you are working on. If the dog keeps standing every time he gets into the *sit* position, keep gently manipulating him back into the *sit*. It is imperative that you make him stay in the *sit* position for a moment or two after you say "Stay." Be sure to reward the dog and progress with the *stay* in very small steps so that it's easy for the dog to understand.

I want to talk about the elevated area where you've been training your dog to sit and stay. Whether you're training your dog on a chair, a couch, a table, a porch, or any other elevated surface, it serves as a *designated and defined place*, which makes things easier for your dog.

The elevated training area makes things easier for your dog, which in turn makes things easier for you.

I do not train my dogs to stay on the flat ground, as it doesn't provide a designated and defined place. Without a designated area for training, it is easy for your dog to cheat. He may scoot his rear end on the ground or even get up and start walking toward you. Early on in training, we need to make things as easy on the dog as possible; in this case, we make it easier for the dog to succeed by taking away much of his ability to cheat.

When you're beginning to train your dog to stay on something that's elevated, and you back away and get some distance, there's really only one mistake that your dog is going to make: jumping off the elevated area. Of course, your response will be to take him back to the area again and ask him to sit and stay. You've just made this pretty simple for your dog: if he jumps off the elevated area, he will be taken back and made to sit and stay.

Let's say you were to train your dog to sit and to stay on the flat ground, as many people do. If your dog were to get up and walk toward you, and you were to take him back to the area and repeat the *sit* and *stay* cues again, your dog will be confused as to why he's being corrected. In his mind, the correction could be for:

- **Getting up from the *sit* position.**
- **Getting up and walking two steps toward you.**
- **Getting up and walking almost all the way to you.**

Not knowing what he's being corrected for is very confusing for a dog, and it can make it harder for him to figure out what you are trying to teach. The elevated area not only makes it easier for your dog to respond correctly to your cues but also eliminates any misunderstandings about your instructions and corrections.

Uses of the *Sit/Stay*

Be certain to incorporate the *sit/stay* into your everyday life. Before you walk out the door, place your dog in a *sit/stay*. Before you feed your dog, make sure that he sits. Have your dog sit and stay when guests are entering your home. By having your dog do the *sit/stay* amid all sorts of distractions and in different situations, you will find that he becomes more and more reliable with the behavior.

While the following *stay* training method is the same for dogs of all colors, the reward system is different. If you are training a dog who can take a treat without getting too out of control (Blue, Green, Yellow, and some Orange), you will use treat rewards. If treats are too much for your dog (Red and some Orange), use petting to reward him. Treats are the preferred method, so if your Orange dog will take treats without becoming too excited, by all means use them.

By following the previously outlined method of teaching your dog to sit, you've already laid a great foundation for the *stay*. Remember, you've said "Stay" each time you've told your dog to sit. Right now, your dog should already be sitting and then staying for a short period of time on the elevated training area with you standing right in front of him.

There are two things to think about when training your dog to stay: *time* and *distance*. Once you have your dog sitting and staying for a few seconds with some consistency, you can begin to slowly extend both the time and distance for which your dog stays in the *sit* position. This is where you need to be creative based on how your dog is progressing.

TIME

Start by setting some goals for yourself. If your dog is consistently staying for two or three seconds after he sits, try to extend it to five seconds. When the dog is staying for five seconds consistently, the next day try for ten seconds. Increase the time a little more each day, and always make sure that you walk to your dog and reward him where he is staying. Remember to keep the training sessions short so that they're fun and interesting for the dog. They do not need to be any longer than a minute or two.

DISTANCE

If your dog is consistently staying when you're 1 foot away from him, try to back up a little more and have the dog stay from 2 or 3 feet away. Once the dog is staying from 2 or 3 feet away from you, try the exercise the next day from 5 or 6 feet away. When your dog is consistent at any given distance, increase it a little more the next day. No matter how far away you are, remember to always walk slowly and carefully to your dog to reward him for staying.

At first, you will be giving the stay cue from right in front of your dog, as simply getting him to remain in position is your first priority.

TIME AND DISTANCE

As your dog begins to get consistent with various lengths of time and different distances, begin to practice both time *and* distance. Don't be afraid to mix things up a bit. If your dog sits and stays from 15 feet away, periodically reward him for sitting and staying from only 4 or 5 feet away. Once your dog is consistent at this distance, you can

As you increase the distance between you and the dog, be ready to grab the leash if needed to put him back into position.

The more you practice, the more reliable your dog will be with the sit/ stay as you increase both time and distance.

move him onto flat ground. Even if your dog sits and stays consistently for thirty seconds at a time, every once in a while reward him after just five seconds. By doing this, you make training interesting for your dog, and, most importantly, you do not become predictable. Eventually, your dog will be sitting and staying from a distance of 15 or 20 feet for at least thirty seconds. At this point, you can consider the behavior trained.

11 teaching *heel*

A few years back, a young woman contacted me for help with her German Shepherd. The dog refused to heel on the leash and delighted in lunging like a maniac. It's bad enough when a Pug or Sheltie refuses to heel on lead; when it's a dog of close to 100 pounds, the problem is serious.

The woman told me that a friend had recommended using redirection with the dog, and she'd been trying it for months with no results. (As we've discussed in previous chapters, redirection is a technique of using food to direct the dog's attention away from a distraction or bad behavior.) To figure out what was going wrong, I watched the woman walking her dog.

At they moved forward, the dog would yank on his leash for four or five seconds, then stop and look up at his owner. In response, she'd give him a liver snap. He'd happily swallow the treat, then lunge forward again and repeat the whole sequence. The woman thought she was rewarding him for the part of the walk when he was *not* pulling, but in fact she was rewarding him for the *entire chain of events*. To the dog's way of thinking, he was being rewarded for tugging, stopping, and looking back at his owner. What a great game, and what an easy, fun way to get a tasty treat!

When you are working with a dog, you must always try to put yourself in his shoes (even if he doesn't wear them). How will he perceive what you're doing? If a dog is barking for twenty-five seconds and then stops and you give him a treat, clearly the dog thinks that you enjoyed his twenty-five-second monologue and he'll subsequently repeat it, maybe even louder! Rewarding a dog after he's jumped up on you will make the dog think that jumping on people is a good thing. So don't reward a dog instantly when he stops a bad behavior—dogs know that you don't get cookies for doing nothing.

Not every problem or behavior can be accomplished with redirection or a reward. Positive training techniques work in many scenarios, but sometimes correction is required to teach the dog what is expected.

Getting Started

Once your dog is trained to sit and stay, I recommend teaching the *heel.* This cue is tremendously important because it teaches the dog appropriate boundaries and that he must look to you for direction; it's also great exercise for the two of you. For years, I have taught this behavior with a certain technique in classes, on television, and in DVDs. This is the first time I've put this training technique in print. I hope you find it simple and easy to understand. Please remember to take it slow and work at your dog's pace, just as you would when working on any behavior.

Sometimes to really learn how to do something right, you need to understand how it is done wrong. Over the years, I have seen dogs trained to heel incorrectly more often than I've seen them trained correctly. Two of the most common mistakes are that the wrong tools are used and that corrections are administered inappropriately.

Let's first talk about the right tools. If you have a Red or Orange dog who wants to pull, use a chain choke collar for the *heel.* When used properly, the chain collar will give you a lot of necessary control over the energetic, excitable, warm-colored dogs. For a more fearful dog who does not pull, you will likely be fine with the dog's everyday flat buckle collar. With a Yellow dog, start off with his flat buckle collar; if he seems to be pulling too much once you start training, switch to a chain collar.

The part of the chain collar that attaches to the leash should be on the outside, rather than the inside, of the dog.

When it comes to administering corrections, there are several points you should bear in mind. First, you should not restrain the dog nor should you pull hard on the leash; this is unnecessary and will only encourage the dog to pull back harder. You want to give the leash just a small tug for correction. If you're using a chain choke collar, you should be sure that it releases quickly.

To be sure that you're using the chain collar correctly, look at the collar where it attaches to the leash and follow it down. If the dog is facing away from you, the part that attaches to the leash should be going along the outside of the dog. When you correct the dog, all of the pressure comes from the outside, making the correction much easier to administer. If the collar were on the dog the wrong way, the pressure would come from inside and under him, as you'd be effectively lifting him up to make a correction.

When you administer a correction, you also want the dog to be as close to you as possible; he should not be ahead of you. You must correct the dog before he walks away from you. One reason a dog gets out ahead of his owner has to do with the speed of the person's movement. Think about the basic physics. If you begin walking at normal speed, and your dog is walking with you on leash, the dog naturally will be moving at the same pace as you are. If you are walking at a normal speed and you slow down, the dog will continue moving forward. When you go to correct the dog, he will be ahead of you, which is a bad position for correction. Why is this a bad position? There are three major problems:

1. **Because the dog is several feet in front of you, it is hard for him to decipher why he is being corrected.**

2. **With the dog so far ahead of you, the correction will be much harder for you to deliver, requiring more strength to be effective.**
3. **Because the correction can be severe at this distance, you risk hurting the dog.**

To understand my philosophy on the *heel* cue, you have to know how I interpret this training from the dog's perspective. You will see as you teach your dog to heel that you are teaching your dog an attitude. What you want to impress upon the dog from the very beginning of training is that he needs to stay close to your leg and pay attention because at any time you could make a right, left, or about turn. Unpredictability is the key here. You must constantly change things up so the dog never knows when you are going to stop, speed up, slow down, or start walking in a different direction. At the same time, you also want to make things as easy as possible for the dog.

The position from which we start *heel* training has the dog on leash, standing on your left side, facing in the same direction as you are. You want to make sure that the dog's head is either next to,

You can see how a correction will be both difficult and ineffective with the dog out ahead of you, pulling on the leash.

or in back of, your leg. For that reason, I would not use a head halter or any similar device that goes around the dog's muzzle to teach the *heel*. When you see a dog wearing one of these devices, he is already standing 12 to 18 inches in front of the owner.

Have your dog in position at your left side, even with your leg, before you start to turn.

Step 1: Left Turns

You'll do this first step in your training sessions over the first three or four days. You need only a 4-foot-by 4-foot area.

Start with your dog on leash in the *heel* position. As you say "Heel," pivot your left foot and start to turn counterclockwise; as the dog is on your left side, he will be on your inside as you turn. As you turn, gently pull the dog back with small corrections if he starts to get in front of your leg. Keep rotating counterclockwise, making small corrections as needed until you have made a full revolution. When you complete the revolution, take the time to give your dog a nice tactile reward.

If you notice from the photos, the dog never gets a chance to get in front of my leg. Because of this, the corrections are minimal, which makes it easier for you and easier for your dog. The dog will begin to understand that when you say "Heel," you are going to make that counterclockwise rotation.

After a few sessions, you will not have to correct the dog nearly as much. You will also see the dog taking his own initiative to back up as you make the counterclockwise rotation with your foot. You are making progress! Keep practicing until you barely have to use any corrections to make that one revolution.

ABOVE: Begin a left turn by pivoting your left foot outward. BELOW, LEFT: As you turn left (counterclockwise), the dog will be on your inside.

Step 2: Right Turns

This step is going to take you into the next few days of training sessions; you can use the same training area as you did in Step 1. Start with your dog in the same position as you did in Step 1. As you say "Heel," pivot your right foot clockwise and gently pull the dog toward you with small corrections. You may need to correct your dog a little more emphatically because the dog is now on your outside, and you are pulling the dog into you.

Keep rotating clockwise until you have made a full revolution; again, be sure to give that tactile reward at the end of the revolution.

While the corrections may be firmer than in Step 1, they should still be small, because even though you are pulling the dog toward you, you are moving very slowly. Keep practicing until you see the dog keeping himself in the proper position on his own, without any corrections, as you turn. Your goal is to make a full revolution without correcting the dog at all.

Step 3: Mixing It Up

When your dog is consistent turning in both directions, it's time to start mixing it up. Say "Heel," turn clockwise, and then turn counterclockwise. Remember what we discussed earlier—once you start walking at a normal pace (which you are not doing now), your dog

With right (clockwise) turns, the dog will be on your outside and more likely to lag behind, so it may take more effort on your part to keep him even with your leg.

This is the position you want your dog to be in as you do a right turn. He's even with your leg and walking at your pace.

will be moving at that same pace. If you slow down, the dog will continue moving forward. The best thing to do when that happens is an about turn, which means that you change directions quickly. Your dog will need to turn and walk with you because he is on a leash and has no choice.

As you practice changing directions in your small training area, you will find yourself making figure-8s as you change from clockwise turns to counterclockwise turns and vice versa. Have fun with your practice sessions, and give your dog plenty of tactile rewards for a job well done.

Step 4: Moving Forward

This is the fun part, but also the part where owners can get a false sense of security. As your dog starts to move forward, you want to create an attitude in him of having complete control of himself. You are going to accomplish this by taking one ridiculously slow step forward. It should take three seconds from the time your left foot leaves the ground to the time it touches again. I've seen many of my clients go way too fast, so you may want to practice without the dog to get a feel for how slow you need to go. This is the key to training this behavior. It sounds funny, but the dog has no choice but to walk slowly because of your extremely slow pace. Here is what you'll do:

- **Take one very slow step forward and follow it with a counterclockwise revolution, then take another very slow step forward and follow it with a counterclockwise revolution.**
- **If your dog walks too far out to the side of you, just give a gentle tug, tell him to "Heel," and bring him closer to you**
- **Repeat this for the next five training sessions.**
- **The next phase is to take several steps forward, still keeping that same ridiculously slow speed. Change things up by making both clockwise and counterclockwise turns.**
- **If things are going well, you can start taking even more steps forward in between your turns, still staying very slow.**

Step 5: Changing Speeds

Once your dog is in control of himself when you're moving slowly, you can start to change speeds. You want the dog to know that you could slow down to that ridiculously slow speed at any time; this keeps the dog in control. You will say "Heel" *only once* when you start to walk. Walk in a straight line very slowly for about 3 feet, then speed up to a normal pace, and then slow down again, following the speed change with a turn to the left or right. If the dog veers off or lags behind, give a quick correction followed by "Heel." The more time you spend practicing, the more reliable your dog will be. Once the behavior is trained, all you should need to do is say "Heel" at the very beginning as you start moving.

index